SMALL *Oxford* BOOKS

THE PLEASURES
OF THE TABLE

Also by Theodora FitzGibbon

SMALL *Oxford* BOOKS

THE PLEASURES OF THE TABLE

Compiled by
THEODORA FITZGIBBON

Oxford New York Toronto Melbourne
OXFORD UNIVERSITY PRESS
1981

Oxford University Press, Walton Street, Oxford OX2 6DP

London Glasgow New York Toronto
Delhi Bombay Calcutta Madras Karachi
Kuala Lumpur Singapore Hong Kong Tokyo
Nairobi Dar es Salaam Cape Town
Melbourne Wellington

and associate companies in
Beirut Berlin Ibadan Mexico City

British Library Cataloguing in Publication Data

The Pleasures of the table — (Small Oxford books)
1. Food habits — Literary collections
I. FitzGibbon, Theodora   II. Series
809'. 93355   PN6071.F6   80-42092

ISBN 0-19-214120-1

*

For my dear friend
John Tovey
who has given me so many
'pleasures of the table'

Printed in Great Britain by
Hazell Watson & Viney Limited
Aylesbury, Bucks

Introduction

Of all the arts the culinary is perhaps the most ancient, and it is clear that, from earliest times, it has been of great importance to mankind, not merely as an aid to nutrition, but as a means of self-expression and creative endeavour. Over the millennia, it has exercised the imaginations of kings and commoners, prelates and poets, as well as philosophers and people who simply want to make their everyday lives more interesting by tasting a new food or drink.

There are few things more rewarding than food, and the pleasure is available to many, for good food does not necessarily mean expensive food. It is enjoyed by all nationalities and it is interesting to note that a feast is often the prelude to difficult negotiations between one country and another. Food is considered the essential part of a special occasion such as a wedding or an anniversary.

Food as such is, however, not enough. It must be well prepared, suitable to the occasion, and the atmosphere and the company must be in harmony. This is truly the pleasure of the table: a repast prepared with affection, if not with love.

It is for this reason that I am more concerned in this book with the harmony of eating, rather than eating itself, for the latter is common to all living creatures, and depends largely on hunger. The true pleasure is the personal choice, into which the care, knowledge, and imagination of the host or hostess plays a very large part. We have all experienced the rich glow of satisfaction after a meal spent in pleasant company, something which is sadly lacking if the company is not *sympathique*. For the most simple repast of good bread and cheese with a glass of wine in the company of a loved friend can be a memorable occasion.

This simple experience is found all through the ages. People's attitude to food has always been the same, as is shown markedly in these pages. If some of the meals chosen seem of gargantuan proportions, do not immediately think of gluttony, for remember that even at the beginning of this century almost everybody took far more exercise. The daily round of the parson or doctor was done on horseback; the running of even a small household entailed the cleaning and filling of endless lamps, coals being brought long distances, and much more walking, not only for the daily providing, but also to visit friends. In 1802 Dorothy Wordsworth thought little of walking the thirteen miles or so from Grasmere to Keswick to visit Coleridge, and later Southey and his family, not only by the road, but sometimes along the moorland track which strikes from Thirlmere to Watendlath, and so by Ashness Bridge on to the Borrowdale Road, which was then nearly two miles from Greta Hall. Such walks were not considered unusual and at the end of them a good meal would have been almost a necessity, and a pleasure with her friends.

It must also be remembered that the lavish table of the eighteenth century, covered, as it now seems to us, with endless dishes, was more in the manner of a modern buffet. No one was expected to eat of everything: the choice was there and one took what one wanted. Most of it was done in the spirit of hospitality, to produce of one's best as much as all could possibly want and to let them enjoy it together in the chosen company.

All these things I have attempted to illustrate throughout the ages; that food, although one of the necessities of life, is a pleasure which we can all enjoy, and it should be one of the everyday things that makes life worth living. I have not, in the text, quoted from the Bible, but here I will:

> A man hath no better thing under the sun,
> than to eat, and to drink, and to be merry.
>
> Ecclesiastes 8:15

I hope that this little book will promote such enjoyment.

T.F.

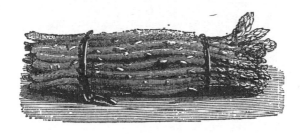

THE PLEASURES OF THE TABLE belong to all ages, to all conditions, to all countries and to every day: they can be associated with all the other pleasures and remain the last to console us for the loss of the rest.

Jean Anthelme Brillat-Savarin, 1755–1826

Few would dispute the truth of Brillat-Savarin's witty words for they summarize the thoughts of all gastronomes since earliest times. Food was to be enjoyed and revered, as well as acting as sustenance for both body and mind.

Food is better than power. . . . If a man abstain from food for ten days, though he live, he would not be able to see, hear, perceive, think, act and understand. But when he obtains food, he is able to see, hear, perceive, think, act and understand.

The Upanishads or Vedanta, 4th Vol. of the Indian Philosophical Work, *c.* 1500–600 BC

The Chinese

Food has always been of immense importance in Chinese culture and an interest in food is as old as that culture itself. When Duke Long of Wei asked Confucius (551–478 BC) about military tactics, he replied:

I have indeed heard about matters pertaining to *tsu* (meat stand) and *tou* (dish of meat) but I have not learned military matters.

Lun yu (ed.), *Confucian Analects*

It is said according to Shih chi and Mo Tzu, that I Yin, the Prime Minister of King T'ang of Shang (a ruler of the T'ang dynasty, 907–618 BC), was originally a cook, and

THE PLEASURES OF THE TABLE

*that it was his culinary skills that brought him to T'ang's
notice and favour. Of the nearly 4,000 people responsible
for running the King's palace, 60 per cent of them had
to do with preparing food and wine for ritual meals and
pleasureable gatherings. Poems were written about delicious
food and drink to lure back the soul of the departed.*

Oh soul, come back! Why should you go so far away?
All your household have come to do you honour: all
     kinds of good food are ready:
Rice, broom-corn, early wheat mixed with yellow millet
Bitter, salt, sour, hot and sweet: there are dishes of all
     flavours.
Ribs of the fatted ox cooked tender and succulent;
Sour and bitter blended in the soup of Wu;
Stewed turtle and roast kid, served up with yam sauce;
Geese cooked in sour sauce, casseroled duck, fried
     flesh of the great crane;
Braised chicken, seethed tortoise, high seasoned, but
     not to spoil the taste;
Fried honey cakes of rice flour and malt sugar
     sweetmeats;
Jade-like wine, honey-flavoured, fills the winged cups;
Ice-cooled liquor, strained of impurities, clear wine,
     cool and refreshing;
Here are laid out the patterned ladles, and here is
     sparkling wine ...

    Chao Hun, *The Summons of the Soul* (Chou dynasty, 12th
                 cent. BC–221 BC)

During the Han dynasty (206 BC–AD 220) a passage from
Contract for a Slave *(T'ung-yueh) by Wang Pao, gives
the slave these instructions for the preparation of a dinner
for guests:*

When there are guests in the house he shall carry a kettle
and go after wine; draw water and prepare the evening

meal; wash bowls and arrange food trays; pluck garlic from the garden; chop vegetables and mince meat; pound meat and make stew of tubers; slice fish and roast turtle; boil tea and fill the utensils.

The Egyptians

The ancient Egyptians raised certain vegetables to the rank of goddess (the radish) and gods – the leek, onion, and particularly the cabbage. All had altars raised to them and prayers were offered up each day.

... they are the only people among whom it is custom at their feasts to eat boiled cabbages before all the rest of the food.

So wrote the Egyptian Athenaeus (2/3 cent. AD), who lived in Greece and was the author of a fifteen-volume work on dinner-table philosophers and banquets called the Deipnosophistai.

Perhaps the cabbage was eaten first because of what the Greek botanist Theophrastus discovered:

... the vine as long as it lives always turns away from the smell of cabbage!

Beer was certainly the general drink of the ancient Egyptians but there was also a delicious wine, drunk by the rich, called Mareotic, which was made from grapes grown near Alexandria, which Athenaeus said was:

... white and sweet, and good for the breath and digestible.

Archestratus was a Greek poet (c. 330 BC) who travelled widely in search of foreign delicacies for the table, as a result of which he wrote a humorous poem which was freely translated by Ennius, called Heduphagetica. *About*

300 lines are preserved in Athenaeus's book, and these are his rules for a civilized Greek meal:

> I write these precepts for immortal Greece,
> That round a table, delicately spread,
> Or three, or four, may sit in choice repast,
> Or five at most. Who otherwise shall dine,
> Are like a troop marauding for their prey.

The Ancient Greeks

The heroes of Greek legend fared well, the food being of the simple but solid variety, unlike the elaborate delicacies of Imperial Rome.

Patroclus . . . put down a big bench in the firelight and laid on it the backs of a sheep and a fat goat and the chine of a great hog rich in lard. Automedon held these for him, while Achilles jointed them, and then carved up the joints and spitted the slices. Meanwhile Patroclus, the royal son of Menoetius, made the fire blaze up. When it had burnt down again and the flames had disappeared, he scattered the embers and laid the spits above them, resting them on dogs, after he had sprinkled the meat with holy salt. When he had roasted it and heaped it up on platters, Patroclus fetched some bread and set it out on the table in handsome baskets; and Achilles divided the meat into portions.

Homer, *The Iliad*

The favourite wine of those days according to Homer was Pramnian. In The Iliad *the Lady Hecamede serves it to Nestor and Machaon:*

. . . an onion to eat as a relish with the drink, some yellow honey, and sacred barley-meal; and beside these a magnificent beaker adorned with golden studs. . . . In

[4]

this cup, their comely attendant mixed them the pottage with Pramnian wine and, after making it ready by grating into it some goat's-milk cheese with a bronze grater and sprinkling white barley on top, she invited them to drink, which they did.

The variety of foods enjoyed is well described in Teleclides' Amphictyons *where the delights of Paradise are envisaged.*

The streams all ran with rosy wine, and barley cakes fought with wheaten loaves to be the first to reach a hungry man's open mouth. . . . Fish too came straight to men's doors and fried themselves, all ready, dished themselves up, and stood upon the table before the guests. A stream of soup flowed along in front of all the couches, bearing with it chunks of smoking-hot meat. And rivulets of white sauce brought to all who chose to eat, the sweetest forcemeat balls. . . . Dishes there were of boiled meat too, and sausages and pastries. Roasted thrushes and forcemeat balls flew down men's throats as if spontaneously. There were sounds too, of cheesecakes champed in hungry men's jaws, while young ones picked over pieces of tripe and paunch and liver.

The Romans

Unlike the quick-witted Greeks, who were able to entertain each other by anecdotes, reminiscences, tales grave or gay, the Romans had to be entertained by paid singers, dancers or clowns, somewhat on the lines of the 'Cabarets' of modern times . . . .

The Romans were greater eaters than the Greeks, but not such great talkers . . . .

Joseph Vehling, *Apicius: Cookery and Dining in Imperial Rome*

In Imperial Rome three couches (for three people each) were arranged in a U shape, called the triclinium, *and guests (their shoes removed) reclined around it, the food being set in the middle of the U. After an early breakfast the Romans had a light collation about midday. Seneca tells us that 'a little bread and a few figs were all that my virtue requires'. Dinner or supper was the main meal which invariably took place at the ninth hour (3–4 p.m.), but many were also served with another meal about midnight* (commissatio). *This particularly appealed to the gluttonous Emperor Vitellius, who according to Suetonius, 'thought nothing of snatching lumps of meat or cake off the altar, almost out of the sacred fire, and bolting them down'. Vitellius dedicated a dish to the goddess Minerva made from pike livers, pheasant brains, peacock brains, flamingo tongues and lamprey roe.*

§

However, not all banquets were so exotic or elaborate. The poet Martial writes of a dinner offering many herbs and vegetables.

My bailiff's wife has brought me mallows, to aid digestion, and other treasures of the garden. Among them are lettuces and leeks for slicing; and there is no lack of mint – the antidote to flatulence – and the stimulant elecampane. Slices of egg will crown anchovies dressed with rue, and there shall be sow's teats

swimming in tunny sauce. These will act as whets for
the appetite. My little dinner will all be placed on the
table at once. There will be a kid snatched from the
jaws of a rapacious wolf; there will be small pieces such
as do not need a carver; there will be beans and young
cabbage sprouts. To these will be added a chicken; and
a ham which has already appeared at the table three
times. For dessert I will give ripe fruits.

*Food was highly thought of in ancient Rome. Aurelian
remarked to Flavius (c. 330 BC):*

Take care, take care above all things that the markets
of Rome be well supplied: nothing more gay or peaceful
than the people when they are well fed.

*Seneca describes the luxury of the table among Epicurean
Romans.*

Behold Nomentanus and Apicius, those happy con-
querors of all that is delectable on earth or in the sea.
Behold them at table, stretched on their couches, and
contemplating innumerable viands. Harmonious songs
flatter their ears, a variety of pleasing objects occupy
their eyes, and the most exquisite savours captivate
their insatiable palates.

*(Apicius, who lived in the first century AD. was a gourmand
who wrote books on cooking. According to Seneca, after
spending a fortune of about 100 million sesterces mainly
on food, on finding that he had only 10 million left, he
poisoned himself.)*

The genius of gluttony multiplied the banquets by
prescribing luxurious gastronomic assemblages, sometimes in honour of the gods, and often for the gratifi-
cation of simple mortals themselves.

Alexis Soyer, *The Pantropheon*, 1853

Banquets were offered to Jupiter in the Capitol, and to the goddesses Juno, Minerva, and Ceres. Soyer remarks:

These divinities were splendidly served, and as they touched nothing, in the middle of the night the seven epulary priests joyously ate the supper of the immortals.

There were triumphal banquets given by the victors. After the conquest of Asia many new foods appeared, including spices and cherries brought by Lucullus to Rome. Nowadays Lucullus is remembered more for his banquets than for his great military achievements. He converted the garden of his house on the Pincio in Rome into a fine series of terraces growing many fruits, and he also bred thrushes, a favoured food of the time. Plutarch wrote of him:

The life of Lucullus was like an ancient comedy, where first we see great actions, both political and military, and afterwards feasts, debauches, races by torchlight, and every kind of frivolous amusement.

Suetonius said that the downfall of the Roman Empire was due to the apathy and gluttony of the people. Many emperors did their best to control gluttony. Julius Caesar made great efforts to restrict the purchase of food, and he stationed guards at the markets with orders to seize whatever they found in contravention of the strict laws. Augustus tried to modify the laws and permitted gatherings of twelve persons in honour of the twelve great gods, and the expenditure of about eight shillings on ordinary repasts; twelve shillings on the banquet of the Calends, the Ides and the Nones; and even two pounds on wedding days and the day following. Tiberius relaxed these edicts allowing four pounds for a supper. Suetonius relates that the magistrates had to restrict the amount of food offered for sale in eating houses and cooking shops, even banning bread. And to set an example Tiberius sometimes served left-over dishes from the day before – or only one side of a wild boar, which he said contained everything that the other side did. But Caligula, Claudius and Nero undid all the good and allowed everyone the right to ruin themselves as pleasantly as they pleased.

As an act of justice to Pagan legislators we are compelled to say that sometimes they had excellent views. . . . The laws of Minos prescribed to the Cretans the annual levy of an impost, the half of which was to be consecrated to the nourishment of the people. No one could eat alone; a certain number of families met together to take their repasts in common. At Lacedaemon, each one brought his share of the provisions necessary for the supper as a whole, or he sent at the commencement of the month to the steward of the common halls, wine, cheese, figs, a measure of flour, and a small sum of money to defray other expenses. Friendship, sobriety, and concord presided without exception at these meetings.

Alexis Soyer, *The Pantropheon*, from Plutarch

Cooking and Preserving

In the so-called Dark Ages many foods underwent refinement. The Arabs purified sugar, and the Venetians had a particular talent for crystallizing salt.

During the many invasions of Europe by the Barbarians the preservation of food was important.

In the famous Venetia, fish alone is abundant; rich and poor live there on equal terms. A single food nourishes all alike . . .

Cassiodorus, AD 500

Venice gained much of her commercial supremacy by the

[9]

salting of fish, and later meat, which was exported in return for cloves and other spices from the East.

§

Development in the colder northern climates was much slower. Pytheas of Marseilles, a contemporary of Alexander the Great, wrote a description of his voyage up the west coast of Britain, to the Orkney and Shetland Islands. He wrote that the climate of Britain was foggy and damp and the people grew great quantities of corn.

§

The cooking of meats by roasting and stewing became easier in Europe after the introduction of metal for cauldrons was adopted from Greek trading colonies. These vessels of riveted sheet bronze were seen and copied by the Irish about the eighth or seventh century BC.

The eating habits of the Celts in Gaul have been described by Posidonius (135–51 BC), and they were, no doubt, the same in parts of Britain and Ireland.

The diners were waited on by their elder children and sat on straw or skins on the ground and ate the meats with their hands in a cleanly but leonine fashion, raising up whole limbs in both hands and biting off the meat, while any part which is hard to tear off they cut through with a small dagger which hangs attached to their sword sheath in its scabbard. . . . Beside them are hearths blazing with fire with cauldrons and spits containing large pieces of meat. Brave warriors they honour with the finest portions of the meat. . . . They are exceedingly fond of wine and the merchants provide it. . . .

The Romans in Britain had an early breakfast (often before dawn) of bread and fruit – then a light midday meal of fish, eggs and vegetables, at which wine and water was drunk. There was a native beer although many Romans disliked it. A poem written by the Emperor Julian in the fourth century attacks it thus:

ON WINE MADE FROM BARLEY

Who made you and from what?
By the true Bacchus I know you not.
He smells of nectar,
But you smell of goat.

Dinner began in the late afternoon and consisted of several courses.

Early Britain

The grinding of corn, barley, oats and rye and the making of bread was common from the early Iron Age, the Celtic settlers in Britain having developed a clay dome for baking, and the Romans introduced their bread ovens into Britain. Butter-making was also introduced into Britain by the Celts during the pre-Roman Iron Age, and they were noted as coopers. Pliny described their butter-making, and says they considered it their choicest food, '. . . the one that distinguishes the wealthy from the lower orders'. Butter was usually salted, as was the cheese: 'You would lose all your butter and cheese, were I not at hand to protect it for you', claims the salter in Aelfric's Colloquy.

In Ireland the butter was often preserved in the bog, and in Wales cheese was marinated for a time in brine. A section of early Welsh divorce law laid down division of property as such:

The provisions are thus to be shared: to the wife belong the meat in the brine, and the cheese in the brine; and after they are hung up they belong to the husband; to the wife belong the vessels of butter in cut, the meat in cut, and the cheese in cut. . . .

In the life of St Finian of Clonard (in Ireland) we are told:

Now this was his daily refection – a bit of barley bread and a drink of water. On Sundays however, and on holydays, a bit of wheaten bread and a piece of boiled salmon.

The ninth-century anonymous Irish poet in 'The Hermit's Song' writes of less frugal fare:

> ... I will choose and will not hide it,
> Fragrant leek,
> Hens, salmon, trout and bees.

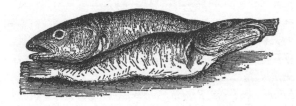

Of Conall the Red, a wealthy Connacht landowner, it was said:

Never, too, was his house without the three sacks, to list, a sack of malt for preparing yeast, a sack of wheat for preparing the refection of the guests, and a sack of salt to make every food taste well.

In the Irish law tracts, a passage from the Senchus Mor *cites the foods given to the children:*

The children of the inferior grades are fed to bare sufficiency on stirabout made of oatmeal on buttermilk or water, and it is taken with stale butter. The sons of the chieftain grades are fed to satiety on stirabout made of barley meal upon new milk, taken with fresh butter. The sons of kings are fed on stirabout made of wheaten meal upon new milk, taken with honey.

Abbot Eginhard, the Emperor Charlemagne's Secretary, gives us a good idea of his eating habits.

His daily meal was served in four courses only, exclusive of the roast, which the hunters used to bring in on spits, and which he ate with more pleasure than any other food.

In the ninth century a monk of the St Gall monastery recorded this of one of Charlemagne's banquets:

... while Charles was eating, he was waited upon by dukes and rulers, and Kings of various peoples; and when his banquet was ended then those who served him fed, and they were served by counts and prefects and nobles of different ranks. And when these last had made an end of eating, then came the military officers and scholars of the palace, then their subordinates, then the servants of those servants. So that the last comers did not get a mouthful of food before the middle of the night.

His estates were divided into units each run by a steward who had to supply the emperor with 'clear and methodical accounts'. Each Christmas 'The produce of the vegetable and kitchen gardens were sold and brought in considerable revenue'.

The Middle Ages

In the thirteenth century the food was unvaried and the contrast in diet and consumption between rich and poor was enormous. In the autumn, when cattle had to be killed for smoking or salting to provide winter food, there was a glut, and those who could afford it were extravagant in their feasts. In readiness for Christmas at Winchester

*Castle in 1206, King John ordered the Sheriff of Hamp-
shire to procure 1,500 chickens, 5,000 eggs, 20 oxen,
100 pigs and 100 sheep!*

Beef is a good meate for an Englysshman so be the
beest be yonge. . . . Olde beef and cow flesshe doth
ingender melancolye humoures. [Yet] . . . if it be
moderately powdeyd and the grose blode by salte be
exhawtyed it doth make an Englysshman strong.

from a 14th-century manuscript

*However, it was not available to all, as in the fourteenth-
century poem* Piers Plowman, *Langland writes of the
near-famine period for the poor before harvest-time when
'cold flesh and cold fish is to them like baked venison'.*

I haven't a penny to buy pullets or geese or pigs, but
only two green cheeses, a few curds and cream and an
oaten cake, and two loaves of beans and bran baked
for my little ones. By my soul I haven't any salt bacon,
nor even any eggs, by Christ, to make ham-and-eggs.
But I have parsley and leeks and many cabbages, and
also a cow and a calf, and a mare to cart my dung while
the drought lasts. By these means must we live till
Lammas time [1 August] and by then I hope the crops
in my field will be ripe. Then I can prepare the dinner
the way I like best.

Passus VI

*Chaucer's lecherous merchant January is definite in his
choice:*

'Old fish and young flesh is what I like. A pike is
better than a pickerel, and better than old beef is
tender veal.'

The Merchant's Tale from *Canterbury Tales*

Fish was a most vital food obtainable at all times of the year.

Fysshe, the which is in ryvers and brokes, be more holsome than they be in ponds and mootes, or other standing water, for they doeth labour and doth skower themselves. Fysshe and els that do feede in the fen or morysshe ground doth saver of the moude.

Andrew Boorde, 1542

Elis and lampurnes rosted where that everye go
Cast vinegre and powder thereon furst get the *bonus*
them fro.

ibid.

[i.e *roasted eels and lampreys should have vinegar and spiced salt ('powder') put on them to bring out the goodness*]

Dame Juliana Berners, Abbess of Sopwith c. 1470, and the supposed authoress of Treatyse of Fysshynge, *entreated all noblemen to refrain from fishing in the poor men's private waters and from breaking the gins in the weirs to steal the fish caught in them. Dame Juliana's list of fish caught mentions salmon – 'the most stately fish that any man may angle to in fresh water', trout, grayling, barbel – 'a sweet fish, but it is a queasy meat', carp, cherin or chub, bream, tench, perch, roach, dace, bleak, ruff, flounder, minnow, eel, and pike.*

Every so often the large ponds were culled and the fish sorted out.

The mill-pond. And in the seventh year of the king, twenty-eighth day of January [1467/8], I brake mine greatest pond in the park, and out of that I took in sixty-five great breams, and I put them into the mill-pond which is new made, and I put the same day into the same pond, twelve score little carps. And at the same time I put in forty-three great tenches, twenty small tenches, sixty-six small bream, thirteen score of roaches, six score of perches. All these are at this hour and day in the mill-pond.

Manners and Household Expenses, 15th century

Shellfish were popular with both rich and poor, and were particularly welcome during Lent. Dame Alice de Bryene of Acton Hall, Suffolk, sent to Colchester every Sunday for oysters. On 19 March 1413 she ordered for dinner:

. . . four wash [an eighth of a bushel] of oysters, one wash of mussels bought at Colchester, together with the expenses of a groom of the kitchen, and his two horses fetching the same 13*d*; three hundred whelks 9*d*.

Dame Alice also bought a quarter of a barrel of salted sturgeon to last a year, and four barrels of white herrings.

§

Sixteenth-century breakfasts in Lent could be very substantial. The Northumberland Household Book lists the provisions appointed for some of the meals of the family of Henry Algernon Percy, 5th Earl of Northumberland, c. 1512.

My lord and my lady. . . . First a loaf of bread in trenchers, 2 manchets, a quart of beer, a quart of wine, 2 pieces of salt fish, 6 baconned herring, 4 white herring or a dish of sprats.

Nine barrels of red herring were laid in for Lent and five casks of white herring. Also 2,080 salted salmon to last the Percy family until Whitsun.

Salmon has for many centuries been the king of fish. Maestro Martino, Cook to the Most Reverend Monsignor the Chamberlain and Patriarch of Aquileia, who wrote a recipe book c. 1450–75 called De Honesta Voluptate et

Valetudine *(for many years attributed to Platina), says of it:*

Salmon is a most agreeable fish, most natural boiled, and yet again it is good anyway you like to cook it. . . . For whole fish, you need big dishes like my master has, because all fish are much better cooked whole rather than in pieces.

This is sound advice still to be followed today.

§

In the Middle Ages the poor were so poor that on all holidays food was the chief source of enjoyment. Drink was cheaper and more accessible than food. Christmas was a time of feasting for all. This is a contemporary account of Henry VII's Christmas in 1486 which he kept at Greenwich Palace:

The table at which the King sat was richly decorated and groaned beneath the good fare placed upon it; for there was brawn, roast beef, venison pasty, pheasants, swan, capons, lampreys, pyke in latimer sauce, custard, partridge, fruit, plovers and a huge plum pudding which required the efforts of two men to carry. Afterwards plays were performed and there was much music and dancing, and in the large kitchens after the spit had stopped its ceaseless turning, and the King had dined, a merry crowd gathered.

§

A farthing's worth of mussels or a farthing's worth of cockles were a feast for them on a Friday.

William Langland, *The Vision of Piers Plowman*, 14th century

The Meat Eaters

Boar's head or brawn was a great British Christmas speciality for poor and rich alike. It was a delicacy and the centre-piece of many a medieval feast. In the thirteenth century it appeared in the last course along with the game birds, but fifty years later it was served at the beginning of the meal. At the enthronement of Archbishop Nevill in 1467 the feast opened with 'brawn and mustard'.

> Hey! Hey! Hey! Hey!
> The Boar's head in hand I bring,
> With garlands gay in carrying,
> I praye you all with me to sing
> Hey! Hey! Hey! Hey!
>
> Hey! Hey! Hey! Hey!
> Lords and Knights and Squires,
> Parsons, priests and vicars,
> The Boar's head is the first mess!
> Hey! Hey! Hey! Hey!
> The Boar's head is armed gay.

14th century song

William Harrison wrote of the preparation of brawn in Elizabeth I's reign:

It is made commonly of the forepart of a tame boar . . . then sodden in a lead or cauldron . . . till they be so tender that a man may thrust a bruised rush . . . through the fat . . . .Afterward, putting it into close vessels, they pour either good small ale or beer mingled with verjuice and salt thereto till it be covered, and so let it lie . . . till occasion serve to spend it out of the way.

A Court Dinner in 1575 consisted of all the meats beloved of the English.

FIRST COURSE
Pottage of Stewed Broth
Boyled Meat
Chickens and Bacen
Powdered Biefe
Pies and Coffers

Pigge
Rosted Beefe
Rosted Veale
Custarde

SECOND COURSE
Rosted Lamb
Rosted Connies
Chickens
Pea Hennes
Baken Venyson Tarte

from Dorothy Hartley, *Food in England*, 1954

Captain, later Sir, Martin Frobisher describes a croft in the Orkneys in 1577.

Their houses are very simply builded of Pibble Stone, without any chimneys, the fire being made in the midst thereof. The good man, wife and children, and the other of the familly eate and sleepe on the one side . . . the cattel on the other . . . their fire is turffes and cow-shards. They have corn, bigge [hard corn] and oates, with which they pay rent (to the island King). They take great quantity of fish, which they dry in the wind and sun. They dresse their meat without salt. . . . They have egges . . . and fowle . . . their bread is eaten in cakes, their drink is ewe's milk, and in some parts ale . . .

from Dorothy Hartley, *Food in England*

*Meat, and particularly beef, has always been the English-
man's favourite food, the pig being the poor man's source,
usually in the form of bacon, while cattle was the prero-
gative of the rich. Such was their consumption that many
visitors from abroad remarked on it.*

I always heard that they (the English) were great
flesh-eaters, and I found it true. I have known people
in England that never eat any bread, and universally
they eat very little: they nibble a few crumbs, while
they chew the meat by whole mouthfuls. . . . Among
the middling sort of people they have 10 or 12 sorts of
common meats which infallibly take their turns at their
tables, and 2 dishes are their dinners: a pudding for
instance, and a piece of roast beef.

Memoirs of M. Misson, c. 1690

*The English taste was almost emulating that of the
Homeric heroes.*

I pray you, where in Homer is the chief
Who e'er eat fish, or anything but beef?
And, though so much of liberty they boasted,
Their meat was never anything but roasted!

Athenaeus, *Deipnosophistai*

*Samuel Pepys in his diary for 6 January 1662, bears
out M. Misson's words:*

. . . and we had, besides a good chine of beef, and other
good cheer, eighteen mince pies in a dish.

Both meat and pudding are combined in the traditional English steak-and-kidney pudding. In the seventeenth century the Cheshire Cheese tavern in the city produced a pudding between 50 and 80 lb. in weight which took from 16 to 20 hours to boil:

Entombed there-in, beefsteaks, kidneys, oysters, larks, mushrooms, and wondrous spices and gravies, the secret of which is only known to the compounder.

Beer or wine was drunk with such a pudding, depending upon both purse and palate.

§

In July 1665 Samuel Pepys wrote in his diary:

7th At this time I have two tierces of claret, two quarter casks of Canary, and a smaller vessel of Sack, a vessel of Tent, another of Malaga, and another of white wine all in my wine-cellar together . . .

The poet Philip Massinger regales us with a description of an astonishing City of London banquet around 1630 in his play The City Madam.

Men may talk of country Christmases and court
    gluttony,
Their thirty pound buttered eggs, their pies of carps'
    tongues,
Their pheasants drenched with ambergris, the carcases
Of three fat wethers bruised for gravy to
Make sauce for a single peacock: – yet their feasts
Were fasts compared with the City's.

*   *   *

There were three sucking pigs served up in a dish,
Took from the sow as soon as farrowed,
A fortnight fed with dates and muskadine,†

†A much esteemed wine.

That stood my master in twenty marks a piece,
Besides the puddings in their bellies made
Of I know not what.

Act II, i

*For Louis XIV (1643–1715), whether he dined in public
or private, the table was always served in the same manner.*

AT DINNER

2 Large Terrines of Soup
2 Middling Sized Ones
2 Small ones as Side Dishes

FIRST COURSE
2 Large Dishes
2 Middling Sized Ones
6 Small Ones, as Side
  Dishes

SECOND COURSE
2 Large Dishes of Roast
2 More as Side Dishes

As an everyday fare the Dauphin took for his dinner a
nice pottage, with leeks and cabbage, a piece of beef,
another of salt pork, a dish of 6 hens or 12 pullets,
divided in two, a piece of roast pork, cheese and fruit;
at supper, a piece of roast beef, a dish of brains,
neat's feet with vinegar, cheese and fruit. The Barons
of the court had always the half of the quantity of the
Dauphin; the Knights the quarter; the Equerries and
Chaplains, the eighth. The distributions of wine and
bread were made in the same proportions; . . . so that
the young and delicate baroness had four pots of wine,
while the chorister and the chaplain had but one.

Monteil, *Histoire des Français*

*With such sturdy solid food it is interesting to find that
Louis XIV regarded the fork (which had been used for
many years in ducal banquets in Venice and Rome) as a
superfluous luxury, as did his courtiers. The same
obtained in England, where a knife and fingers were*

[22]

thought perfectly respectable eating implements even during the reign of Queen Anne. It was common too for the guests to share the dishes and wine cup between them.

The Irish

A letter written by the Dean of Fermo who accompanied the Papal Nuncio Jean Baptist Rinuccini to the ill-fated Confederation of Kilkenny in 1645 gives an interesting description of the social life of the Irish in Kenmare, Co. Kerry.

The courtesy of the poor people amongst whom my Lord, the Nuncio, took up his quarters was indescribable. A fat bullock, two sheep, and a porker were instantly slaughtered, and an abundant supply of beer, butter and milk was brought to him . . .

Of his own welcome he writes:

They conducted me to one of the nearest huts where I was seated on a cushion stuffed with feathers and the mistress of the house, a venerable old dame, sat down beside me, along with her daughters. A large quantity of delicious milk was then brought to me in a wooden vessel . . . I drank copiously of it, and was quite revived by the draught. . . .

§

They are perpetually pledging healths, the usual drink being Spanish wines, French claret, most delicious beer, and most excellent milk. Butter is used on all occasions. . . . There is also plenty of fruit, as apples, pears and plums, and all eatables are cheap. A fat ox costs 16 shillings, a sheep 15 pence; a pair of capons or fowls, 5 pence, eggs, a farthing apiece. You can have a large fish for a penny. . . . Birds may also be killed with sticks and especially thrushes, blackbirds and chaffinches. . . .

translated by the Rector, later Cardinal Cullen,
of the Irish College, Rome, 1845, where the only
copy is extant in the archives

Vegetables

Green vegetables are seldom mentioned in any accounts of British food up to the seventeenth century, although herbs and the onion family were used for both flavour and medicine, dried peas and beans for potage. The salad given in The Forme of Cury [Cookery] *1390, for the instruction of the cooks of Richard II of England, consists almost entirely of herbs and the onion family.*

Take parsley, sage, garlic, cibols [Welsh onions], leeks, borage, mint, porette [a young leek or onion], fennel, and to them add cresses, rue, rosemary and purslane. Lave them clean, pick them and pluck them small with thine hands and mynge them well with raw oil. Lay on vinegar and salt and serve forth.

An honest laborious countryman, with good bread, salt, and a little parsley, will make a contented meal with a roasted onion.

John Evelyn, 1620–1706

The English cultivated scarcely any vegetable before the last two centuries. At the commencement of the reign of Henry VIII neither salad, nor carrots, nor cabbage, nor radishes, nor any other comestibles of a like nature, were grown in any part of the kingdom; they came from Holland and Flanders.

Anderson, 1548

'Tis scarce a hundred years since we had cabbages out of Holland, Sir Arthur Ashley, of Wilburg St Giles, in Dorsetshire, being the first who planted them in England. . . .

Cabbage is not so greatly magnified by the rest of the doctors, as affording but a gross and melancholy juice. Yet loosening, if moderately boil'd. It is seldom eaten raw, except by the Dutch.

A Gardener's Book of 1699

The potato (both sweet and Virginian) was first used in sweet dishes:

A tart that is a courage to a man or woman. (*1596*)

Mashed potatoes were mixed with herbs, spices, dates, wine, sugar, egg yolks and brandy, then set in pastry.

Sir Francis Drake said this of the sweet potato:

These potatoes be the most delicate rootes that may be eaten, and doe farre exceed our parseneps or carets. Their pines be of the bignes of two fists, the outside whereof is of the making of a pineapple, but it is soft like the rinde of a Cucomber, and the inside eateth like an apple but it is more delicious than any sweet apple sugred.

The potato was not generally used as a vegetable in Ireland except by the very poor, until the late eighteenth or early nineteenth century.

Seldom was the potato used at the farmer's or cottier's table unless during the winter or close season of the year, and this at dinner only.

Royal Irish Academy O.S. Memoirs,
Dungiven, Co. Londonderry, 1834

Scotland cultivated many vegetables in the early eighteenth century.

He [Mr Holmes of Johnstown, Co. Kildare, Ireland] has not for five or six years past been without a small field of Scotch cabbages.

Arthur Young, A Tour in Ireland, 1776–9

On the continent Catherine de Médicis married the Dauphin (later Henry II of France) in 1533 and brought her own cooks with her. Later Marie de Médicis' cooks introduced new vegetables such as broccoli, Savoy cabbages, and globe artichokes, along with new ways of cultivation.

In 1660 the first petit pois *were brought from Genoa and presented to Louis XIV where they were an immediate success at the court.*

... impatience to eat them, the pleasure of having eaten them, the joy of eating them again, are the three questions which have occupied our princes for the last four days. There are ladies who, having supped, and well supped, with the King, go home and there eat a dish of green peas before going to bed ... it is a fashion, a fury ...

from a letter by Madame de Sévigné 1626–96

Coffee Drinking

Nathaniel Conopios, about whom John Evelyn remarks that he saw him drinking coffee at Balliol College in 1637, is said to have been the first to bring the custom to England from Turkey. The earliest English coffee-house was established at The Angel in Oxford in 1650. Two years later London opened its first coffee-house in St Michael's Alley, Cornhill, and many others soon followed. In 1663 they were allowed to sell alcoholic drink at the cost of not more than 1d. per glass. This pre-dates the first French coffee-house which an Armenian called Pascal opened at the Easter St Germain Fair in 1699.

Moderately drunk it removes vapours from the brain, occasioned by fumes of wine, or other strong liquors, eases pains in the head, prevents sour belchings, and provokes appetite. . . . In a word, coffee is the drunkard's settle-brain, the fool's pastime, who admires it for being the production of Asia, and is ravished with delight when he hears the berries grow in the deserts of Arabia, but would not give a farthing for a hogshead of it if it were to be had on Hampstead Heath. . . .

T. Tryon, *The Good Hous-wife Made a Doctor*, 1692

Drinking Chocolate

After the British captured Jamaica in 1655 a direct trade in cocoa beans started. In 1657 the drink chocolate was sold in Queen's Head Alley, Bishopsgate, London, and was advertised as

. . . an excellent West India drink called chocolate to be sold, where you may have it ready at any time, and also unmade at reasonable rates.

It was not always highly thought of. In France Madame de Sévigné recorded:

The Marquise de Coëtlogon took so much chocolate, being pregnant last year, that she was brought to bed of a little boy who was as black as the devil!

Chocolate or coffee was the breakfast drink of the gentry, taken with toast or spiced bread. But by the late eighteenth century both were enjoyed less and less as tea became the important new drink.

Tea Drinking

Although tea had been known for centuries in China it was used mainly as a flavouring for rice cakes. The infusion in boiling water came about in the fifteenth century, and in 1664 the East India Company brought small amounts of ch'a *directly to England from China and Malaya. The Portuguese, who had founded a trading station at Macao, also sent some tea back to Portugal, but it was all extremely expensive.*

§

Tea-drinking became an assured success when the Portuguese wife of Charles II, Catherine of Braganza, encouraged it at court.

Genuine cups or dishes and china tea-pots were imported ; metal urns which could be heated in drawing-rooms, and later the tea-kettle, became fashionable. Tea-parties became the rage, and the expensive cost of tea added a note of snobbery to the proceedings. It also helped to spread the habit, and the first tea-shop for ladies (coffee-houses were for men only) was opened by Thomas Twining in Devereux Court, London, in 1717. In 1732 the Vauxhall Pleasure Gardens were opened as a tea-garden where members of both sexes could drink tea and enjoy concerts and spectacles, and the success of Vauxhall opened up many more such gardens in and around London.

Hollands, punch, claret drawn from the wood at 3/6*d* a quart, skittles and quoits offered their fascinations to the male customers; while the ladies and juveniles were beguiled with cakes and ale, tea and shrimps, strawberries and cream, syllabubs and junkets. . . .

Tom Brown, *Bygone Pleasures of London*

The almond cheesecakes will be always hot at 1 o'clock as usual; and the rich seed and plum cakes sent to any part of the town at 2/6*d* each. Coffee, tea and chocolate at any time of the day; and fine Epping butter may also be had.

Mr Trusler, Marylebone Gardens,
Daily Advertiser, May 1760

The best varieties of tea could only be bought by the rich, but cheaper tea was sold which had been smuggled from the continent. Even the respectable Parson Woodforde was not above buying it. He wrote in his diary for 29 March 1777:

Andrews the Smuggler brought me this night about 11 o'clock a bagg of Hyson tea 6 Pd [pounds] weight. He frightened us a little by whistling under the Parlour Window just as we were going to bed. I gave him some Geneva and paid him for the tea at 10/6*d* per Pd.

Tea seems to have been introduced into Scotland by Mary of Modena, wife of James II, who held court at Holyrood in 1681. By the eighteenth century 'afternoon' tea was the thing, and the products of the national gift for baking were part of the ceremony.

When I was a boy, tea was the meal of ceremony, and we had fifty-odd kinds of tea-bread. One Scot made a little fortune by his milk-bakes. His shop in Forrester's

Wynd was surrounded at 5 o'clock by a great concourse
of servant maids. . . .

Henry Mackenzie, *The Man of Feeling*, 1771

*Not all Scotsmen approved of tea-drinking; in 1729,
Mackintosh of Borlum comments on the changed times:*

When I come to a friend's house of a morning, I
used to be asked if I had my morning draught yet. I
am now asked if I have had my tea. And in lieu of the
big *Quaigh* with strong ale and toast, and after a dram
of good wholesome Scots' spirits, there is now the tea-
kettle put to the fire, the tea-table and silver and china
equipage brought in, and marmalade and cream!

Nor indeed Englishmen!

When will this evil stop? . . . Your very Chambermaids
have lost their bloom, I suppose by *sipping tea?*

Jonas Hanway writing in 1757

*Yet the English tea remains: high tea as a substantial
meal in the north ; afternoon tea as a more genteel social
occasion in the south.*

*The actress Mrs Siddons regaled one such tea-party
with readings from* Macbeth:

After her first reading the men retired to tea. Whilst
we were all eating toast and tinkling cups and saucers,
she began again. It was like the effect of a Mass bell at
Madrid. All noise ceased: we slunk to our seats like
boors, two or three of the most distinguished men of
the day, with the very toast in their mouths, afraid to
bite. It was curious to see Lawrence [the painter Sir
Thomas] in this predicament, to hear him bite by
degrees, and then stop for fear of making too much
crackle, his eyes full of water from the constraint, and
at the same time to hear Mrs Siddons' 'eye of newt and

toe of frog!', and then to see Lawrence give a sly bite, and then look awed and pretend to be listening.

Benjamen Robert Haydon,
Correspondence and Table Talk, 1876

Breakfast

Breakfast was another meal which had quite changed in character. In the country house it took place between 9 and 10 a.m., with sherry and a biscuit being taken at around eleven o'clock. In many houses it was a light meal of tea, coffee, or chocolate with toast, rusks, or cakes but in the Highlands of Scotland it was a very hearty meal in the eighteenth century.

Waverley found Miss Bradwardine presiding over the tea and coffee, the table loaded with warm bread, both of flour, oatmeal, and barley meal, in the shape of loaves, cakes, biscuits, and other varieties, together with eggs, reindeer ham, mutton and beef ditto, smoked salmon, marmalade, and all the other delicacies which induced even Johnson himself to extol the luxury of a Scotch breakfast above that of all other countries. A mess of oatmeal porridge, flanked by a silver jug, which held an equal mixture of cream and buttermilk, was placed for the Baron's share of this repast.

Sir Walter Scott, *Waverley*, 1814

But neither tea nor coffee appears on the Highland breakfast table in Tobias Smollett's Humphry Clinker *(1771)*:

One kit of boiled eggs; a second, full of butter; a third, full of cream; an entire cheese made of goat's milk; a large earthen pot, full of honey; the best part of a ham; a cold venison pasty; a bushel of oatmeal, made into thin cakes and bannocks, with a small wheaten loaf in the middle, for the strangers; a stone bottle full of whiskey, another of brandy, and a kilderkin of ale. There was a ladle chained to the cream kit, with curious wooden bickers [beakers] to be filled from this reservoir. The spirits were drunk out of a silver quaff [*quaich*], and the ale out of horns. Great justice was done to the collation by the guests.

Shooting and fishing induced a large appetite for breakfast in Ireland at the turn of the century.

The Sportsman's breakfast: first, a large bowl of salmon soaked in vinegar – a very common dish this . . . and a bottle of Port wine.

And a little later on when the day's sport was in full swing, liquid refreshment was taken.

In the middle of the table are two glass flagons, each containing about a gallon of whiskey, and everyone proceeds to use, what are significantly termed *(par excellence)* 'the materials'.

A *Sportsman in Ireland*, by A Cosmopolite, 1897

Faujas de St Fond, the King of France's Commissioner for Wines who visited Scotland in the 1780s, commented thus on the breakfast table at the house of Maclean of Torloisk on the island of Mull in 1784:

Table elegantly covered with . . . plates of smoked beef,

cheese of the country and English cheese, fresh eggs, salted herrings, butter, milk and cream; a sort of *bouillie* of oatmeal and water, in eating which each spoonful is plunged into a basin of cream; milk worked up with yolks of eggs, sugar and rum; currant jelly, conserve of myrtle, a wild fruit that grows among the heath, tea, coffee, three kinds of bread (sea biscuits, oatmeal cakes, and very thin and fine barley cakes); and Jamaican rum.

Large breakfasts were also eaten on the Continent:

I went yesterday . . . to breakfast with the Duke de Broglie. There was no cloth upon the table. . . . There was roast fowl, spinach, eggs, apples, wine, and afterwards they brought tea. . . . The children drank wine for their breakfast.

Reverend Sydney Smith (1771–1845)

Sydney Smith did not approve of the Duke's breakfast for when he went again a week later he wrote:

They are virtuous, sensible, disagreeable people, and give bad breakfasts without a table-cloth.

He would without doubt have approved of Brillat-Savarin's breakfast for his relative Doctor Dubois aged seventy-eight, and a military friend aged seventy-six, in 1801.

'Come round tomorrow, at ten o'clock, military time' [under such instructions the first dish must be served as the clock strikes, and all late-comers are regarded as deserters]. At the appointed hour my two guests appeared, newly shaved and carefully combed and powdered; two little old men still hale and hearty.

They smiled with pleasure when they saw the table ready, a white cloth, three places laid, and in each place two dozen oysters, with a bright golden lemon in their midst. A tall bottle of Sauterne stood at each end of the table, carefully wiped except for the corks, which indicated in no uncertain manner that a long time had passed since it had been drawn. . . . After the oysters, which proved admirably fresh, came the broiled kidneys, a jar of truffled *foie gras*, and the *fondue* [scrambled eggs with cheese].

The ingredients were all ready in the saucepan, which was placed on the table over a spirits-of-wine burner. I officiated on the field of battle and none of my movements escaped my cousin's notice. . . . After the *fondue* came fresh fruit and preserves, a cup of real Mocha made *a la Dubelloy* [a new method] and finally two different kinds of liqueur, a detergent spirit, and a soothing oil.

When breakfast was well and truly over I proposed a little exercise in the form of a tour of my apartment, which, though far from elegant, is both vast and comfortable, and where my friends felt all the more at home in that the ceiling and gilding date from the middle of the reign of Louis XV.

These gargantuan breakfasts postponed the dinner hour to about 4 p.m., and in England the meal could consist of:

. . . part of a large Cod, a Chine of Mutton, some Soup, a Chicken Pye, Puddings and Roots. Second course, Pidgeons and asparagus. A Fillet of Veal with Mushrooms . . . rosted Sweetbreads, hot Lobster, Apricot Tart, and in the middle a Pyramid of Syllabubs and Jellies. We had a Dessert of Fruit after Dinner and Madeira, White Port and Red to drink as Wine.

Then there would be a supper at about ten o'clock probably consisting of cold meats!

A surviving eighteenth-century Irish menu lists the following foods:

1ST COURSE – Fish, beefsteaks, rabbits and onions, soup, fillets of veal, blancmange, cherries and Dutch cheese.

2ND COURSE – Turkey, grilled salmon, quails, little terrine peas, mushrooms, leveret, crab and cheese-cakes.

3RD COURSE – A selection of fruits: currants, goose-berries, strawberries and raspberries with cream; sweetmeats and jelly, almond cream and orange butter.

The Clergy

Not only the gentry and country squires ate and drank well, but also the country parsons. Parson James Wood-forde (1740–1803) gives accounts of many a good dinner in his Diary.

Oct. 12 [1770] . . . Mrs Carr, Miss Chambers, Mr Hindley, Mr Carr, and Sister Jane dined, supped and spent the evening with me, and we were very merry. I gave them for dinner a dish of fine Tench which I caught out of my brother's Pond in Pond Close this morning, Ham, and 3 Fowls boiled, a Plumb Pudding; a couple of Ducks rosted, a roasted neck of Pork, a Plumb Tart, and an Apple Tart, Pears, Apples and Nutts after dinner White wine and red, Beer and Cyder. Coffee and Tea in the evening at six o'clock. Hashed Fowl and Duck and Eggs and Potatoes etc. for supper. We did not dine till four o'clock – nor supped till ten. Mr Rice, a Welshman who is lately come to Cary and plays very well on the Triple Harp, played to us after coffee for an hour or two . . . the Company did not go away till near twelve o'clock . . .

My Father's maid Betty dressed my dinner etc. with my People. The dinner and supper were extremely well done and well set of.

Parson Woodforde's interest in food is surprising, for he not only grew a lot of vegetables such as artichokes, cauliflowers, cucumbers, and fruit, but he also kept pigs. All this he noted daily in his Diary.

Another innovation was the rotation dinner which helped to keep up the standards. The rotation dinner club was organized amongst the neighbouring clergy and their wives, all of whom dined in turn at each other's houses. These dinners were larger than when the family ate alone, and the table was set with a large dish at each end, and four smaller ones in the centre. The corners consisted of vegetables and sweet dishes.

May 14 [1782] . . . It being my Rotation Day, Mr and Mrs Bodham, Mrs Davy, Mr Howes and Mr Du Quesne dined and spent the Afternoon with us . . . I gave my Company for Dinner, 4 Spring Chickens boiled and a Ham, part of a Rump of Beef boiled, a Leg of Mutton rosted with Sweet Sauce and a boiled Plumb Pudding.

Revd. James Woodforde, *Diary of a Country Parson*

Dinner with the Bishop, Dr Lewis Bagot at Norwich, was a grand affair.

There were 20 of us at the Table and a very elegant dinner the Bishop gave us. We had 2 Courses of 20 Dishes each Course, and a Desert after of 20 Dishes. Madeira, red and white Wines. The first Course amongst many other things were 2 Dishes of prodigious fine stewed Carp and Tench, and a fine Haunch of Venison. Amongst the second Course a fine Turkey Poult, Partridges, Pidgeons and Sweetmeats. Desert – amongst other things, Mulberries, Melon, Currants,

Peaches, Nectarines and Grapes. A most beautiful Artificial Garden in the Center of the Table remained at Dinner and afterwards, it was one of the prettiest things I ever saw....

4 September 1783

The Reverend Sydney Smith (1771–1845), a canon of St Paul's, was a wise, witty cleric who loved not only good food, but also to cook.

'I am convinced' *he wrote*, 'that character, talents, virtues, and qualities are powerfully affected by beef, mutton, pie crust, and rich soups.'

His elder brother married Caroline Vernon, aunt of the 3rd Lord Holland, and he was a most welcome visitor at Lady Holland's table. His ready wit set everyone at their ease. Speaking of the tragedy-queen Mrs Sarah Siddons (1755–1831) he remarked 'that it was never without awe that he saw her stab the potatoes!'

§

In April 1826 Sydney Smith made his first visit to Paris and was enchanted by the cooking. On his second visit in 1835 he wrote to Lady Grey:

I shall not easily forget a Matelotte at the Rocher de Cancale, an almond tart at Montreuil, or a Poulet à la Tartare at Grignon's. . . . These are impressions which no changes in future life can ever obliterate.

When he returned to England he still thought of those meals and wrote to a friend in Yorkshire:

Let me beg of you a greater attention than you have hitherto paid to *Sauce à la Tartare* – it opened to me a new train of ideas. How shall I be able to live upon the large raw limbs of meat to which I am destined? Where shall I find those delicious stews, that thoroughly subjugated meat which opposes no resistance to the teeth, and still preserves all the gravies for the palate? It fills me with despair and remorse to think how badly I have been fed, and how my time has been misspent and wasted on bread sauce, and melted butter.

When Lady Holland sent him some ham from Spain he wrote:

Many thanks for the two fine Gallicia hams; but, as for boiling them in wine, I am not as yet high enough in the Church for that; so they must do the best they can in water!

The Irish cleric's dinner parties were of a simpler variety, but enjoyed nevertheless.

Father Horgan was the soul of hospitality, and gave many a dinner-party, where all sorts and conditions of men were wont to meet: at the upper end of his table were clergy and gentry of the neighbourhood, peasant farmers at the lower. The eatables were alike for all – alternate dishes of chicken and bacon all down the table. With the drinkables it was different; there was wine at the upper end, whiskey (which they preferred) for the farmers at the lower. He said to me, 'You see, my dear friend, I don't know how to order a big dinner with all sorts of dishes; and if I did, old Bridget could not cook it. So I just have a pair of chickens and then a dish of bacon and greens, then another pair of chickens and another dish of bacon and greens, and so on all the way down. Everyone likes chickens and bacon, and when a man sees these before him he looks for nothing else. I am saved a world of trouble, and every one seems happy and contented.' And so they were, and right pleasant those homely dinners were – quite as pleasant as those given by . . . a wealthy solicitor in Dublin, famous for his cook and for the excellence and abundance of his wine, especially his claret.

W. R. Le Fanu, *Seventy Years of Irish Life*, 1894

French Gastronomes

In 1825 the Mayor of Belley, the famous gastronome and gourmand Brillat-Savarin, a cousin of Madame Récamier, published his superb book La Physiologie du Gout, *and everything he says about food is both pertinent and prodigious.*

To entertain a guest is to make yourself responsible for his happiness so long as he is beneath your roof.

It is chiefly people of intelligence who hold gourmandism in high esteem: others are incapable of an operation which consists of a series of judgements and appreciations. . . .

I once attended a dinner of gourmands. . . . Following an admirable first course, there appeared, among other dishes, a huge Barbezieux cockerel, truffled fit to burst, and a Gibraltar-rock of Strasbourg *foie-gras*. This sight produced a marked, but almost indescribable effect on the company. . . . Sure enough, all conversation ceased, for hearts were full to overflowing, the skilful movements of the carvers held every eye; and when the loaded plates had been handed round, I saw successively imprinted on every face the glow of desire, the ecstasy of enjoyment, and the perfect calm of utter bliss.

Brillat-Savarin, trans. Anne Drayton,
The Philosopher in the Kitchen, 1970

There is the following footnote:

A witty woman once said to me that she was able to tell gourmands by their pronunciation of the word *good* in such phrases as 'That's good, that's very good' etc.; she declared that adepts instil into that one short monosyllable an accent of truth, tenderness, and enthusiasm such as ill-favoured palates can never attain.

I wonder what Brillat-Savarin would have made of Mr A's party in Dublin in the late 1880s.

A few days afterwards Chief Justice Doherty, who had been one of the guests, met Mr A –, and said to him, 'What a pleasant party we had with you last Tuesday!'

'Do you call that a pleasant party?' said A–. 'I don't.'

'Why not?' said Doherty.

'Too much talk, too much talk; you couldn't enjoy your wine; you drank a little more than a bottle each. On Wednesday I had nine men to dinner, and they drank three bottles a man; and you'd have heard a pin drop the whole time. That's what *I* call a pleasant party.'

W. R. Le Fanu, *Seventy Years of Irish Life*, 1894

He would certainly have approved of the Prince of Lampedusa's dinner in Sicily in the 1860s.

The Prince was too experienced to offer Sicilian guests, in a town of the interior, a dinner beginning with soup, and he infringed the rules of *haute cuisine* all the more readily as he disliked it himself. . . . So when three lackeys in green, gold, and powder entered, each holding a great silver dish containing a towering macaroni pie, only four of the twenty at table avoided showing pleased surprise. . . .

Good manners apart, though, the aspect of those monumental dishes of macaroni was worthy of the quivers of admiration they evoked. The burnished gold of the crusts, the fragrance of sugar and cinnamon they exuded, were but preludes to the delights released from the interior when the knife broke the crust; first came a smoke laden with aromas, then chicken livers, hard-boiled eggs, sliced ham, chicken and truffles in masses of piping hot, glistening macaroni, to which the meat juice gave an exquisite hue of suede.

The beginning of the meal, as happens in the provinces, was quiet. The arch-priest made a sign of the Cross and plunged in headfirst without a word. The organist absorbed the succulent dish with closed eyes; he was grateful to the Creator that his ability to shoot hare and woodcock could bring him ecstatic pleasures like this. . . .

Prince Giuseppe di Lampedusa, *The Leopard*, 1960

Probably the greatest of all French chefs, Marie Antoine Carême (1784–1833), shared Brillat-Savarin's views on the social importance of food:

When we no longer have good cooking in the world, we will have no literature, nor high and sharp intelligence, nor friendly gatherings, nor social harmony.

[41]

Carême was Talleyrand's chef for some time, and when Talleyrand was going to the Congress of Vienna in 1814 he said:

I have more need of cooked dishes than of written instructions.

In 1815 Carême went to England to cook for the Prince Regent in the Brighton Pavilion, but he did not hold a high opinion of English cooking. His remarks also show that the Englishman's table had not changed since the seventeenth century.

The essentials of English cooking are the roasts of beef, mutton and lamb; the various meats cooked in salt water, in the manner of fish and vegetables . . . fruit preserves, puddings of all kinds, chicken and turkey with cauliflower, salt beef, country ham and several similar ragouts – that is the sum of English cooking.

Lady Morgan writes this of a dinner Carême cooked in 1828 when working for a Monsieur Rothschild:

To do justice to the science and research of a dinner so served would require a knowledge of the art equal to that which produced it . . . every meat presented in its natural aroma; every vegetable in its own shade of verdure.

The plombière *or iced pudding was described thus:*

. . . with the hue and odour of fresh gathered nectarines, [it] satisfied every sense and dissipated every coarser flavour.

Food and Poetry

Certain foods have evoked poetic responses in lovers of good food. Mutton became an eighteenth-century favourite.

> J'aime mieux un tendre gigot
> Qui sans pompe et sans étalage,
> Se montre avec un entourage
> De laitue et de haricots.
> Gigot, recevez mon hommage.
> Souvent, j'ai dedaigné pour vous
> Chez la baronne ou la marquise
> La poularde la plus exquise,
> Et même les perdrix aux choux.
>
> Joseph Berchoux, *La Gastronomie ou L'Homme des champs à table*, 1801

Grimod de la Regnière said: 'Que le gigot soit attendu comme un premier rendezvous d'amour.'
>
> *Almanach des Gourmands*, 1803–10

Dean Jonathan Swift (1667–1745) gives the following instructions on roasting mutton, to be sung to Geminiani's air 'Gently touch the warbling Lyre':

> Gently stir and blow the fire,
> Lay the mutton down to roast,
> Dress it quickly, I desire,
> In the dripping put a toast,
> That I hunger may remove –
> Mutton is the meat I love.
>
> On the dresser see it lie;
> Oh! the charming white and red;
> Finer meat ne'er met the eye,
> On the sweetest grass it fed:

[43]

Let the jack go swiftly round,
Let me have it nicely brown'd.

On the table spread the cloth,
Let the knives be sharp and clean,
Pickles get and salad both,
Let them each be fresh and green.
With small beer, good ale and wine,
Oh ye gods! how I shall dine.

from *The Cook's Oracle* by Dr Kitchener, 1820

Sur le fourneau mijote doucement un ragoût de mouton,
idéal fauve, doré, avec une sauce courte d'une couleur
transparente et chaude, et des pommes de terre pareilles
à des topazes qui seraient vivantes.

Théodore de Banville (1823–91)

Beef had a similar effect on other people.

. . . an old-style beef stew which overwhelmed at least
three senses out of five, for, besides its dark and
velvety flavour, its melt-in-the-mouth consistency, it
shone with a bronze caramelized sauce, ringed around
the very edge with a light golden fat.

'What is this masterpiece?'

'It's beef.'

'But there is in this dish a mystery, a magic. One
should be able to put a name to such a marvel.'

'To be sure', replied Madame Yvon '– it's beef.'

Colette (1873–1954), *Prisons et Paradis*

*Henri Bosco, the early twentieth-century French writer,
writes evocatively of a country* daube *in* Barboche.

A *daube* cooked gently in an earthenware stew pot of
venerable age, for three whole days, the three days
required, and seasoned as it should be, a *daube* of
succulent and well-basted meats, is surely the greatest
of all treasures! Should I decide to swallow it, it is

only when I have savoured it with the most sensitive parts of my mouth that I can distinguish the sharpness of the pepper, the virtues of the garlic, the fineness of the pork fat, the mildness of the onion and the exquisiteness of the thyme, all melted with the steam from the liquid seasoned with little pinches of salt.

The poet William King (1663–1712) eulogizes on the English apple-pie.

Of all the delicates which Britons try
To please the palate or delight the eye,
Of all the sev'ral kinds of sumptuous fare,
There is none that can with applepie compare.

Ranged in thick order let your Quinces lie,
They give a charming relish to the Pie.
If you are wise you'll not brown sugar slight,
The browner (if I form my judgment right)
A deep vermilion tincture will dispense,
And make your Pippin redder than the Quince.

When this is done there will be wanting still
The just reserve of cloves and candied peel;
Nor can I blame you, if a drop you take
Of orangewater for perfuming's sake.
But here the nicety of art is such,
There must not be too little nor too much.

[45]

O be not, be not tempted, lovely Nell!
While the hot-piping odours strongly smell,
While the delicious fume creates a gust,
To lick the o'erflowing juice or bite the crust.

You'll rather stay (if my advice may rule)
Until the hot is corrected by the cool;
Till you've infused a luscious store of cream,
And changed the purple for a silver stream.

Other poets wrote in a more comic vein.

Let *Christmas* boast her customary Treat,
A Mixture strange, of Suet, Currants, Meat,
Where various Tartes combine, the greasy, and the
    sweet.
Let glad *Shrove-Tuesday* bring the Pancake thin,
Or Fritter rich, with Apples stor'd within:
On *Easter-Sunday* be the Pudding seen,
To which the *Tansey* lends her sober Green:
And when great *London* hails her annual *Lord*,
Let quiv'ring *Custard* crown the *Aldermannic* Board.

But BEN prepares a more delicious Mess,
Substantial Fare, a Breakfast for Queen *Bess*:
What dainty Epicure, or greedy Glutton,
Would not prefer his PIE, that's made of *Mutton?*

Each diff'rent Country boasts a diff'rent Taste,
And owes its Fame to *Pudding* or to *Paste*:
SQUAB PIE in *Cornwall* only they can make,
In Norfolk DUMPLING, and in Salop CAKE:
But *Oxford* now from all shall bear the Prize,
Fam'd, as for *Sausages*, for MUTTON-PIES.

  Anon, 'On Ben Tyrrell's Pies' from *The Oxford Sausage*, 1764

Charles Stuart Calverley (1831–84) writes amusingly of vegetables. From his poem Fly Leaves:

> One morning in the garden bed
> The onion and the carrot said
> Unto the parsley group:
> 'Oh, when shall we three meet again,
> In thunder, lightning, hail or rain?'
> 'Alas!' replied, in tones of pain
> The Parsley, 'in the soup.'

Mr Donald McCullough's after-dinner 'Grace' could have been quoted by all of us some time in our lives.

> *If* the soup had been as warm as the claret ...
> *If* the claret had been as old as the chicken ...
> *If* the chicken had been as fat as our host ...
> It would have been a splendid meal.

And so could the following rhyme.

> Oh, the night porter's port
> Is not the same sort
> As the port that is brought by the day porter!
> For the night porter's port's
> Not a port but a tort,
> While the day porter's port's from Oporto.

George Morrison (1922–)

Dining Alfresco

Alfresco meals have always had their charms:

A kettle of fish is a *fête-champêtre* of a particular kind, which is to other *fête-champêtres* what the piscatory eclogues of Brown' or Sannazzaro are to pastoral poetry. A large cauldron is boiled by the side of the salmon river, containing a quantity of water, thickened with salt to the consistence of brine. In this the fish is plunged when taken, and eaten by the company *fronde super viridi*. This is accounted the best way of eating salmon by those who desire to taste the fish in a state of extreme freshness. Others prefer it after being kept a day or two, when the curd melts into oil, and the fish becomes richer and more luscious. The more judicious gastronomes eat no other sauce than a spoonful of the water in which the salmon has been boiled, together with a little pepper and vinegar.

Sir Walter Scott, *St Ronan's Well*, 1824, note

. . . a kettle was placed upon the flat rock beside the fall, and kept full of boiling water. Into this the fish sometimes fell, in their attempts to ascend, and being boiled in the presence of the company were presented to dinner. This was a delicacy in the gastronomical art unknown to Monsieur Ude.

R. Carruthers, *The Highland Notebook*

On a wild spot within the Ballochiebuie Forest, with Lochnagar towering above it, stands one of the most delightful of the Royal Shiels, once a favourite picnic site of Queen Victoria when in residence at Balmoral. The Queen records:

When we came back to the Little Shiel, after walking for an hour, we had tea. Brown had caught some excellent trout and cooked them with oatmeal, which the dear Empress [Eugenie] liked extremely, and said would be her dinner.

Leaves from the Journal of Our Life in the Highlands, 1846–61

The Reverend Francis Kilvert writes of an amusing picnic to Snodhill Castle in the Golden Valley in his Diary *for Tuesday 21 June 1870.*

An attempt was made to build a fire gypsy fashion with three sticks propped together to hold a pot full of new potatoes which nearly proved a disaster.

The Flames soon burnt through one of the supports, and when the fire was at the fiercest down came the three sticks and the pot upside down hissing into the midst of the flames. The pot lid flew off, out rushed the water and potatoes, and a cloud of steam arose from the fire. . . . At length the pot was settled upright upon the embers, more water having been poured in, and another armful of dry wood heaped upon it. . . . Twenty minutes passed . . . while the ladies got flowery wreaths and green and wild roses to adorn the dishes and table cloth spread under an oak tree, and covered with provisions . . . a fork plunged into the potatoes and they were triumphantly pronounced to be done to a turn. Then there was a dispute how they should be treated. . . . They were however poured out on the ground, and then the pot fell upon them, crushing some and blackening others. Eventually the potatoes were handed round. . . . There was plenty of meat and drink, the usual things, cold chicken, ham and tongue, pies of different sorts, salads, jam and gooseberry tarts, bread and cheese. Splendid strawberries from Clifford Priory. . . . Cup of various kinds went round, claret and hock, champagne, cider and sherry, and people sprawled about in all attitudes and made a great noise – Henry Dew was the life of the party, and kept the table in a roar. . . . The ladies wandered away by themselves. At last we all met upon the mound . . . and sat in a great circle whilst the remains of the cup, wine and soda water were handed round. Then we broke up, the

[49]

roll of carriages was heard coming through the lanes below, and everyone seized upon something to carry down the steep, slippery grass slopes.

Brillat-Savarin counts a simple shooting luncheon as one of the most agreeable of repasts.

A shady spot takes his fancy; soft grass welcomes him, and the murmur of the nearby spring invites him to deposit in its cool waters the flask of wine destined to refresh him. Then, with calm contentment, he takes out of his knapsack the cold chicken and golden-crusted rolls packed for him by loving hands, and places them beside the wedge of Gruyère or Roquefort which is to serve as his dessert.

He is not alone during these preparations; with him is the faithful animal which Heaven created to serve him; squatting beside him, the dog looks up with loving eyes at his master; co-operation has brought them closer; they are two friends, and the servant is proud and happy to share his master's meal.

Escoffier's description of a shooting party for about ten people in the valley of the Haute-Savoie in November 1911 is mouth-watering. It begins the evening before the shoot:

Our meal that evening was composed of a cream of pumpkin soup with little croûtons fried in butter, a young turkey roasted on the spit accompanied by a large country sausage, and a salad of potatoes, dandelions and beetroot, and followed by a big bowl of pears cooked in red wine and served with whipped cream.

Next morning at the agreed hour, we were all ready, and furnished with the necessary provisions and accompanied by local guides we climbed the rocky paths, real goat tracks, without too much difficulty . . .

the day promised to be fairly fruitful. And indeed so it turned out since we were back at the house by about 4 o'clock, somewhat tired, but proud to count out: three hares, a very young chamois, eleven partridges, three capercailzies, six young rabbits, and a quantity of small birds.

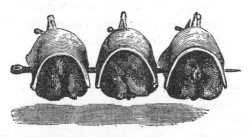

On their return the party had a light meal before dinner. The game bag was hung for subsequent meals.

Our dinner that evening consisted of a cabbage, potato, and kohlrabi soup, augmented with three young chickens, an enormous piece of lean bacon, and a big farmhouse sausage. The broth, with some of the mashed vegetables, was poured over slices of toast, which made an excellent rustic soup. What remained of the vegetables were arranged on a large dish around the chickens, the bacon and the sausage . . . and each of us did due honour to this good family dish.

To follow we were served with a leg of mutton, tender and pink, accompanied by a chestnut purée. Then a surprise – but one which was not entirely unexpected from our host who had an excellent cook – an immense hermetically sealed terrine, which, placed in the middle of the table, gave out, when it was uncovered, a marvellous scent of truffles, partridges and aromatic herbs. This terrine contained eight young partridges amply truffled, and cased in fat bacon, a little bouquet of mountain herbs, and several glasses of fine champagne cognac. All this had been gently cooked in hot embers for some hours. At the same time a celery salad was served. As for the wines, we had first the excellent local white wine, then Burgundy, and finally a famous brand of champagne. The dinner ended with beautiful local fruit and fine liqueurs.

After a hearty breakfast they visited the farm before an early luncheon in the great dining hall, for which they were joined by the mayor and village curé.

Luncheon was composed partly of the trophies of the previous day's shooting . . . nor did we have any *hors d'oeuvre* but instead some *ombres chevaliers* [a char-like fish] from the lac du Bourget, cooked and left to get cold in white wine from our host's own vineyard. These were accompanied by a completely original sauce, and here is the recipe.

Grated horseradish, mixed with an equal quantity of skinned finely chopped walnuts, a dessertspoon of powdered sugar, a pinch of salt, the juice of two lemons, and enough cream to obtain a sauce neither too thick nor too liquid.

After the *ombres chevaliers* we had eggs scrambled with cheese, enriched with white truffles which a shepherd had brought from the boundary of the Savoie, close to the frontier of Piedmont. Then came an excellent civet of hare *à la bourgeoise*, assuredly far superior to all the fantasies known as *à la Royale*. . . . The majestic roast consisted of the capercailzies in the middle of a large dish, surrounded by the partridges, and the small birds, of which we had made the day before a hecatomb.

A superb *pâté de foie gras* sent direct from Nancy was scarcely touched; on the other hand, we did considerable justice to the dessert: the season's fruits and excellent little cream cheeses.

Having risen from table at six o'clock, we once more

found ourselves there, as if by chance, three hours later for a little cold supper; have I not already said that the mountain air is the best of aperitifs?

The following day, which was Sunday, we were obliged, not without regret, to take leave of our hosts, and return home . . . we had a final lunch before our departure. It was composed of eggs and bacon, little galettes of maize flour fried in butter, a terrine of rabbit and cold meats. The chamois had been put to marinate, and would be cooked some days later for other guests. We all carried away with us the happiest memory of this beautiful country of Savoie, and of the very hospitable welcome we had received. For my part, I have never forgotten the horseradish and walnut sauce.

Le Carnet d'Epicure, 1912

Madame, I have only cried twice in my life; once when I dropped a wing of truffled chicken into Lake Como, and once, when for the first time I heard you sing.

The composer Gioachino Rossini (1792–1868), when congratulating the diva Adelina Patti on her singing

When I was going through the course of Garrison instruction, and accustomed to long days out surveying, I was partial to a galantine made of a small fowl, boned and rolled, with a block of tongue, and some forcemeat introduced into the centre of it. A home-made brawn of tongue, a part of an ox-head, and sheep's trotters, well seasoned and slightly spiced, was another *specialité*.

A nice piece of the brisket of beef salted and spiced, boiled, placed under a weight, and then trimmed into a neat shape is a very happy thing for the tiffin basket; and a much respected patron of mine recommends for travelling a really good cold plum pudding, in which a glass of brandy has been included.

'Wyvern' (Col. Kenney Herbert),
Culinary Jottings for Madras, 1885

Travellers' Fare

Travellers' meals are often unexpected, and what Brillat-Savarin calls traveller's luck can often be experienced.

About eleven o'clock in the morning I arrived at an inn in the small town or village of Mont-sous-Vaudrey; and after attending to the wants of my mount I went into the kitchen, where a sight met my eyes which no traveller could have beheld without a thrill of pleasure.

In front of a blazing fire a spit was slowly turning, most admirably decked with kingly quails, and with those little green-footed landrails which are so very plump. This choice game was yielding its last drops on to a huge round of toast, which looked as if it had been fashioned by a sportsman's hand; and close by it, already cooked, lay one of those round leverets which Parisians never see, and the smell of which would scent a church as sweetly as any incense.

'Good', I said to myself . . . 'Providence has not utterly forsaken me. Let me pluck this flower on my way; I can always die a little later!'

Then addressing the innkeeper . . .

'My dear fellow,' I said 'What good things are you going to offer me for dinner?'

'Nothing but good things, Monsieur,' he answered; 'Good *bouilli*, good potato soup, good shoulder of mutton, and good haricot beans.'

At this unexpected reply a shiver of disappointment ran through me: the reader knows that I never eat *bouilli*, because it is meat robbed of its juices; beans and potatoes are both fattening; my teeth, I felt, were not strong enough to tear up mutton; in a word, this menu was calculated to break my heart . . .

'And for whom are you keeping all this fine game?' I asked with an air of extreme annoyance.

'Alas Monsieur . . . it is not mine to dispose of; it all belongs to some legal gentlemen who have been here these past ten days . . . they finished their work yesterday, and are celebrating the happy event with a feast – or revolting, as we say in these parts.'

'Monsieur', I replied after a moment's reflection, 'be so kind as to tell these gentlemen that a man of good company begs, as a favour, to be allowed to join them at dinner; that he will pay his share of the cost; and above all, that he will be profoundly indebted to them . . .'

Nevertheless my heart was beating like that of a candidate in an election, waiting for the last votes to be counted. When the innkeeper reappeared, and informed me that the gentlemen were highly flattered by my proposal, and were only waiting for me to join them before they sat down at table. . . .

What a dinner that was! I will not describe it in detail; but I owe an honourable mention to the superb chicken *fricassée*, such as can only be found in the country, and endowed with sufficient truffles to rejuvenate old Tithonus. . . . The roast has been described already, its taste matched its appearance; it was done to a turn, and the difficulty I had experienced in approaching it further enhanced its savour.

Dessert was composed of a vanilla *crème*, choice cheese, and excellent fruit. All these good things were washed down first with a light garnet-coloured wine, then with Hermitage, and later with a dessert wine as sweet as it was generous; and the whole was crowned with some excellent coffee, confectioned by the sprightly tiler, who also provided us with certain Verdun liqueurs, which he produced from a sort of tabernacle to which he had the key.

Not only was the dinner good; it was also very gay.

La Physiologie du Gout, 1825

Ingenuity was the mother of invention on another of Brillat-Savarin's travels.

One day I was travelling with two ladies whom I was escorting to Melun . . . we arrived at Montgeron with an appetite which threatened destruction to any food-stuffs we encountered. . . . Vain threats: the inn . . . was empty of all provisions; three coaches and two post-chaises had preceded us devouring everything in their path . . . so said the cook.

However, I saw a spit turning in front of the fire, laden with a very handsome leg of mutton. . . . The leg of mutton belonged to three Englishmen, who had brought it with them, and who sat patiently awaiting it over a bottle of champagne.

'But at least,' I said, half in anger and half in suppli-cation, 'couldn't you scramble these eggs for us in the gravy from that leg of mutton? We would be quite content with them, and a cup of white coffee.' 'Why, certainly,' the host replied, 'the gravy is our property by law, and I'll do what you ask at once.' Whereupon he began carefully breaking the eggs.

When I saw that he was fully occupied I went up to the fire, and taking a travelling knife . . . inflicted a dozen deep wounds on the forbidden joint, so its juices should escape to the last drop. I was then careful to join in the business of cooking the eggs. . . . When they were done, I took possession of them and carried them off to the room which had been prepared for my companions and myself.

There we made a feast of them, laughing uproariously to think that we were in fact swallowing all the substance of the mutton, leaving our English friends to chew the residue.

ibid.

Faujas de St Fond, the King of France's Commissioner for Wines, was pleasantly surprised by a meal at an inn in Dalmally, Scotland, in 1784 or thereabouts.

We were astonished at its elegance in so desert a place. . . . Our supper consisted of two dishes of fine game, the one of heathcock, the other of woodcock, a creamy fresh butter, cheese of the country, a pot of preserved vaccinium [bilberries], a wild fruit which grows on the mountains, and port wine – all served up together. It was a luxurious repast for the country.

Madame de Boavet, a French traveller in Ireland, was more critical of Irish food in the late eighteenth century. She disliked the custom 'that will have everything eaten together'. However, she was delighted with the roast mutton and delicious gravy – if not with the sauce for the chicken.

At the other end [of the table] were four of those boiled fowls which would be excellent were they not dishonoured by a white paste with chopped parsley in it – the national sauce.

Thackeray, however, found Irish food much to his liking: of a race-ordinary at Killarney he wrote:

. . . for a sum of twelve shillings, any man could take his share of turbot, salmon, venison, and beef, with port, and sherry, and whiskey-punch at discretion.

W. M. Thackeray, *The Irish Sketch Book*, 1843

He describes a simple dish of fresh salmon trout after a fishing expedition in the following manner:

. . . the herd's cottage before named was resorted to: when Marcus, the boatman, commenced forthwith to gut the fish, and taking down some charred turf-ashes from the blazing fire, on which about a hundredweight of potatoes were boiling, he – Marcus – proceeded to grill on the floor some of the trout, which we afterwards ate with immeasurable satisfaction. They were such trouts as, when once tasted, remain for ever in the recollection of a commonly grateful mind – rich, flaky, creamy, full of flavour. A Parisian *gourmand* would have paid ten francs for the smallest *cooleen* among them; and, when transported to his capital, how different in flavouring they would have been! – how inferior to what they were as we devoured them, fresh from the water to the gridiron! The world had not had time to spoil those innocent beings before they were gobbled up with pepper and salt . . . but enough of this: . . . sufficient to say, they were red or salmon trouts – none of your white-fleshed brown-skinned river fellows.

When the gentlemen had finished their repast, the boatmen and their family set to work upon the potatoes, a number of the remaining fish, and a store of other good things. . . .

ibid.

George Borrow thoroughly enjoyed the food during his travels in Wales.

As for the leg of mutton, it is truly wonderful; nothing so good had I ever tasted in the shape of a leg of mutton. The leg of mutton in Wales beats the leg of mutton of any other country, and I had never tasted a Welsh leg of mutton before. Certainly I shall never forget the first Welsh leg of mutton which I tasted, rich but delicate, replete with juices derived from the aromatic herbs of the noble Berwyn, cooked to a turn, and weighing just four pounds.

George Borrow, *Wild Wales*, 1862

Visitors to London found the chop house an excellent place to eat.

Dolly's Chop House in St Paul's Churchyard, for chops, steaks or a 'cut direct' from the joint, with well-boiled mealy potatoes, is particularly good, and this with excellent wine ought to satisfy anybody who, like the young guardsman, could rough it very well on beefsteaks and port . . .

London at Table, 1851

Indeed Boswell endorses this:

A beefsteak-house is a most excellent place to dine at. . . . My dinner (beef, bread and beer, and waiter) was only a shilling.

London Journal, 1762–3

§

In the early nineteenth century the Peninsular Steam Navigation Company, the parent company of the Peninsular and Oriental Steam Navigation Company, was formed, and was subsequently known as the P and O Line. The passengers received (and still do) the best of food and service as this extract from the Memorandum for the Guidance of Pursers and Stewards-in-Charge on Victualling and Management, 1908, *shows:*

It is not the first object of your work to keep down expenditure, but it is your first duty to see a table of superior quality maintained on board your ship, and your passengers thoroughly well satisfied. It has seldom happened that a really good table was not an economical one, compared to one badly managed, but you must clearly understand that what we now instruct you to secure is first an excellent table, and secondly to combine your efforts in that direction with due economy; and it is the wish of the Directors that you should continually seek to improve the table arrangements on board your ship.

P & O SS *Pera*, Bill of Fare, 14th day of
September 1859

Mutton Broth

Roast Fillet Veal	Sea Pies
Stewed Ducks & peas	Roast Goose
Roast Beef	Compote di Pigeons
Boiled Mutton	Corned Pork
Roast Turkey	Beef Steak Pies
Ham	Stew'd Ox Tongue &
Boiled Fowls	Vegetables
Roast Mutton	Roast Fowls
	Curry & Rice

Stewed Breast of Veal & peas

SECOND COURSE

Fruit Tarts	Sandwich pastry
Apple Charlotte	Jam Puffs
Almond Pudding	Stew'd Quinces
Plum Pudding	Jam Tartlets
Lemon Cheese Cakes	Stew'd Nectarines
Currant Pudding	Fancy Pastry

To this add any quantity of Port, Sherry, Madeira, Claret, and soda water, ale & Stout & desert, also any amount of Spirits you please.

The free drinks were a feature of P & O ships and there was always a supply at hand on the sideboard or swinging trays, even after the stewards retired at night. Some 1,300,000 bottles of wine, spirits, beer and soda water were consumed in one year during the 1860s, pale ale and porter topping the list with 524,250 and 166,109 bottles respectively. Claret came next with 123,059 bottles, then sherry, rum, brandy, port, and gin, with whisky a mere 7,424 bottles.

You wouldn't think that fault could be found with either the menu or the drinks, but in 1866 the Reverend Dr Lang found the viands 'too recherché for his taste', and an Australian squatter on board between Aden and Suez (a stretch of the passage guaranteed to reduce appetites) – after partaking heartily of soup, fowl, turkey, ham, roast joint and preserved game, all with vegetables, and then pastry and dessert, the whole washed down liberally with some excellent wine – remarked: 'Well, when I do get ashore, I hope I shall find some food fit for an Englishman to eat.'

The British traveller then (like very many now) only considered British dishes and cooking as good; and had no time for foreign 'kickshaws' – except that, in the liners of the P & O, even in European waters, dishes of Indian curries . . . with all due and proper accompaniments of chutney, poppadums, and 'Bombay duck', plain and Pilau-rice, were from the first regarded as one of the essentials and never-to-be-missed courses.

Boyd Cable, *A Hundred Year History of the P&O*, 1937

Some mariners' fare was almost heaven-sent:

Taking things by and large, as sailors say, I got on fairly well in the matter of provisions even on the long voyage across the Pacific. I always found some small stores to help the fare of luxuries; what I lacked of fresh meat was made up in fresh fish, at least while in the trade-winds, where flying fish crossing on the wing at night would hit the sails and fall on the deck, sometimes two or three of them, sometimes a dozen. Every morning, except when the moon was large, I got a bountiful supply by merely picking them up from the lee scuppers. All tinned meats went begging!

Joshua Slocum, *Sailing Alone Around the World*, 1900

A Taste of New Orleans

New Orleans is famous for its food, and has been for many years. Gumbo is one of its specialities, described by William Coleman in 1885 as follows:

The great dish of New Orleans, and which it claims the honour of having invented, is the GUMBO. There is no dish which at the same time so tickles the palate, satisfies the appetite, furnishes the body with nutriment sufficient to carry on the physical requirements, and costs so little, as a Creole gumbo. It is a dinner in itself, being soup, *pièce de résistance* and vegetable in one. Healthy, not heating to the stomach, and easy of digestion, it should grace every table.

§

'You must try our Creole cookery,' said Mr Commander. 'It's unique in the world. It is a blend, as our history is a blend, with a zest of the Spanish, the finesse of the French, the piquancy of the West Indies, and even a secret from the Choctaw Indians.'

'Indians humph,' said Father, 'Skinny bunch, munching roots and leaves.'

'Exactly so,' said Mr Commander, 'and if I may recommend our gumbo, you will have the unique

[62]

experience of tasting *filé*, which is powdered sassafras leaves.'

'And what else?' asked Father dubiously.

'Tomato, onion, and green pepper, garlic, bay and thyme, forming the typical Creole sauce; then rice, okra, crab meat, shrimp and oysters.'

'I'll take it,' said Father.

'Or there is our shrimp and oyster jambalaya –'

'Another day,' said Father.

'And our *crème brûlée* to crown the meal . . .'

'Not if you put sugar in it . . .'

'Sugar *in* it!' cried Mr Commander, affronted. 'Barbarous! Sugar *on* it, Sir, a crisp crust of brown sugar to contrast with the chilled cream custard below, that's the only way.'

'Agreed,' said Father.

Carol Truax, *Father Was a Gourmet*, 1965

'Father' was a Judge of the New York Supreme Court at the turn of the century, and also a good judge of food and wine.

§

New Orleans during Lent showed no diminution in culinary standards.

'Permit me to introduce myself, Monsieur – Leon Bertrand Arnaud Cacenave, called Count Arnaud, at your service. Welcome to my establishment. May I help you to make your selection?'

'Fish,' said Father.

'Of course. It's Lent.'

'It's also New Orleans,' said Father.

'Then doubly fish,' returned the Count. 'May I suggest – my own creation, oysters Bienville, named for the founder of our town. Then to follow – *pompano en papillote*?'

'Splendid,' said Father.

The Count soon revealed himself to be a connoisseur of French wines which made an immediate bond. When Father tasted the oysters, in their hot wine-fragrant sauce with the crisp brown crust atop, he was delighted to be able to compliment the creator of this work of art in person. He was sorry to let him go when with a murmured apology the Count left the table. He was delighted when the charming fellow came right back.

The Count came smartly up to the table and set down a bottle in a bucket.

'What's this?' asked Father.

'Lagniappe,' answered the Count.

'What's Lagniappe?' enquired Father, adding with a twinkle, 'Never heard of such a vineyard.'

'Lagniappe', said the Count, 'is an old New Orleans custom. Suppose you go to the market, and buy fish for a *coubayon*, the fishmonger gives you some herbs to flavour it. That's lagniappe. Suppose you go into a bar and order a drink, the bartender passes you cheese and crackers. That's lagniappe.'

'That's free lunch,' said Father.

'And suppose you order a meal in my café, I give you lagniappe too – the wine to drink with it.'

'Very good of you,' said Father. 'But' – he looked at the wine label – 'You don't give everybody Château Latour Blanc 1899 I'm sure.'

'I don't,' admitted the Count with his charming smile, 'but nothing less will do for a *bec-fin* like yourself.'

'And it goes very well,' added Father, 'with your delicious *pompano en papillote*.'

ibid.

Judge Truax finds himself at a temporary disadvantage with chopsticks in Japan.

Now the low table was spread with the next gastronomic experiences he had come for – pink slices of fresh tuna, pale gold crisp-fried tempura, and mounds of snowy rice studded with good things. He was eager to get at it. And what did he have to get at it with? A pair of slippery bone knitting needles!

He glared around at his companions. Mrs Watanabe was skilfully nipping up morsels with her chopsticks. Mother, deft as ever, was copying the gesture. Mr Watanabe was holding his rice bowl up to his chin, and his chopsticks were propelling an endless stream of food neatly into his mouth.

Starving in the sight of plenty, Father abruptly clicked down his chopsticks, inserted his fingers into his capacious vest pocket, and pulled out a spoon – an honest Georgian silver spoon. It was a folding spoon, and Father carried it because Mother thought he might need it to take his tonic with. Since Father considered that if you ate enough good food you didn't need to fill yourself up with quack nostrums the spoon had heretofore been neglected. Now it came into its own as Father dipped it into Watanabe's good dishes with a will. A spoon came in especially handy when a juicy suki yaki followed the tempura!

ibid.

In Europe

Henry James was one of the many distinguished Americans who was very fond of Paris.

I indulged in a cheap idyll the other day . . . dining at what is called in Parisian parlance a *guinguette*. . . . It was a very humble style of entertainment, but the most frantic pursuit of pleasure can do no more than succeed, and this was a success. Your table is spread under a trellis which scratches your head – spread chiefly with fried fish – and an old man who looks like a very high-toned political exile comes and stands before it and sings a doleful ditty on the respect due to white hairs. You testify by the bestowal of a couple of coppers . . . and he is speedily replaced by a lad with one arm, who treats you to something livelier: 'À la bonne heure, parlez-moi de ça!'

Henry James, *Parisian Sketches*, August 1876

The Café Anglais, which closed in 1913, was at that time owned by the grandfather of the present owner of the Tour d'Argent, Monsieur Claude Terrail.

It was opened in 1802, and was renowned for its private dining-room on the second floor called Le Salon du Grand Seize which was reserved exclusively for royalty to entertain their friends of the demi-monde. *Courtesans such as Cora Pearl, La Belle Otero, and Liane de Pongy were all constant visitors. It employed excellent chefs such as Dugléré, who created Sole Dugléré.*

To the Café Anglais did they accordingly repair; and in a few minutes a dish of oysters, a lobster – a broiled fowl – and an *omelette aux fines herbes*, were ready for their discussion in a *cabinet particulier* . . .

G. W. M. Reynolds, *Pickwick Abroad or the Tour in France*, 1839

On 7 June, 1867 a dinner was served there to Tsar Alexander II, the Tsarevitch, Wilhelm I, and Bismarck. It was said to have cost 400 francs a head and a replica of the table, with the original silver, crystal and china, is on the ground floor of La Tour d'Argent.

*Parisians and foreigners alike swarmed to a new café
which sold ice-cream.*

. . . this establishment was so much in vogue that it
was difficult to get an ice there; after the opera and
theatres were over, the boulevards were literally
choked up with the carriages of the great people of the
court and the Faubourg St Germain bringing their
guests to Tortoni's.

Reminiscences and Reflections of Captain Gronow, 1862

*Jeanne Detourbey, Comtesse de Loynes, one of the greatest
French hostesses of* la belle époque, *apart from daily
at-homes, always gave two elaborate dinners a week,
one every Friday, and the other every Sunday. She
supervised every detail of the menu and drove with her
chef to the best markets.*

Cost was no problem, and she imported her game,
fish and fruit from the right provinces in the right
season. Her fowl came from Bourg en Bresse with an
occasional pheasant or grouse sent by a poacher she
knew, hams from Luxeuil, and the only fish allowed
into her kitchen had to be freshly dripping with brine
from the Brittany coast. Fruits were served at lush
prime . . . peaches and pears from the Gironde, apples
from Normandy. Once François Coppée bit into a
melon which wasn't quite ripe and it caused an intra-
salon scandal that lasted for years. The Loynes wine
cellar was famous and the service generous. Before
each guest stood a glass for sherry, a glass each for
white and red Bordeaux, one for Burgundy, another
for Château Yquem, and a goblet for champagne. It
was sufficient to satisfy even the novelist Xavier de
Montepin, an unquenchable drinker, who whenever
offered a choice of two wines, would hold up a glass in
either hand and say 'Volontiers!'

Cornelia Otis Skinner, *Elegant Wits and Grand Horizontals*, 1962

In Sicily at the time of the Risorgimento in the 1860s grand balls were held.

Beneath the candelabra, beneath the five tiers bearing towards the distant ceiling pyramids of home-made cakes that were never touched, spread the monotonous opulence of buffets at big balls: coraline lobsters boiled alive, waxy *chaud-froids* of veal, steely-tinted fish immersed in sauce, turkeys gilded by the ovens' heat, rosy *foie-gras* under gelatine armour, boned woodcocks reclining on amber toast decorated with their own chopped guts, and a dozen other cruel, coloured delights. At the end of the table two monumental silver tureens held limpid soup, the colour of burnt amber.

Huge blond *babas*, *Mont Blancs* snowy with whipped cream, cakes speckled with white almonds and green pistachio nuts, hillocks of chocolate-covered pastry, brown and rich as the top soil of the Catanian plain from which, in fact, through many a twist and turn they had come, pink ices, champagne ices, coffee ices, all *parfaits* and falling apart with a squelch at a knife cleft, a melody in major of crystallized cherries, acid notes of yellow pineapple, and those cakes called 'Triumphs of Gluttony', filled with green pistachio paste, and shameless 'Virgin's cakes' shaped like breasts. Don Fabrizio asked for some of these, and as he held them on his

plate looked like a profane caricature of Saint Agatha.
'Why ever didn't the Holy Office forbid these puddings
when it had the chance? Saint Agatha's sliced-off
breasts sold by convents, devoured at dances! Well!
Well!'

Prince Giuseppe di Lampedusa, *The Leopard*, 1960

*In London the oyster house was popular with all, and
Rule's in Maiden Lane was one of the best:*

And the three young Rules rush wildly about; with
dozens of oysters and pewters of stout.

*In 1848 John Simpson joined the Grand Cigar Divan
in the Strand as a caterer, and it was he who introduced
the large hot joints, and steak-and-kidney puddings to
Simpson's-in-the-Strand, still retaining the Cigar Divan
for smoking only.*

. . . an excellent place where you may dine well for
3/6d, and there is also a Cigar Divan. . . .

You can lounge in the evenings, and have admirable
coffee, a cigar, and newspaper to read in a splendid
well-warmed room for 1/-.

Table Book, 1850

*W. R. Le Fanu, brother of the writer Sheridan Le Fanu,
writes interestingly about the original Beefsteak Club in
the early 1870s.*

The day I was there we were twelve, three of whom
were guests – the late Lord Strathmore, who was, I
think, made a member of the club that evening;
Fechter, the famous actor; and myself. In the middle
of the ceiling, over the dinner-table, was the original
grid-iron, which had been rescued from the ruins of
the theatres out of which the club had been built. In
large gold letters round the grid-iron were the words,
'BEEF AND LIBERTY'. The same words were woven in

the centre of the tablecloth, and engraved on all the plates and dishes, and they appeared again in gold on the wall at the end of the room, through a sort of portcullis in which you saw the beef-steaks being cooked. Over this portcullis were the words, 'IF IT WERE DONE WHEN 'TIS DONE, THEN 'TWERE WELL IT WERE DONE QUICKLY'. With the exception of a welch [*sic*]-rabbit as second course, the dinner consisted of beef-steaks, and beef-steaks only. These came in in quick succession, two by two, one well done, the other rather under-done, so as to suit all palates. The drink was porter and port wine, which went round in flagons. The conversation was general and full of fun.

After dinner the chairman brewed a huge bowl of punch – whether of brandy or of whisky, I forget; the vice-chairman a smaller one of rum. From the bowls jugs were filled, one of which was placed before each of those at table.

. . . the chairman said: 'It is the custom here that the guests shall rise and return thanks simultaneously.' The chairman then rose again and said, 'I now propose that the excellent speeches, which have been delivered by our eloquent guests, be printed and circulated at the expense of the club . . .'

After that, till ten o'clock, 'the night drave on wi' sangs and clatter', when we separated, after as pleasant an evening as I ever spent.

W. R. Le Fanu, *Seventy Years of Irish Life*, 1894

§

The table, so often the forum of wit, can also be the seat of comedy as exemplified in this passage about the poet Coleridge's father, a learned clergyman of Ottery St Mary, Devonshire.

Dining in a large party one day, the modest divine was suddenly shocked by perceiving some part, as he conceived, of his own snowy shirt emerging from a part of his habiliments. . . . The stray portion of his supposed tunic was admonished of its errors by a forcible thrust back into its proper home; but still another limbus persisted to emerge, or seemed to persist, and still another, until the learned gentleman absolutely perspired with the labour of re-establishing order. And, after all, he saw with anguish, that some arrears of the snowy indecorum still remained to reduce into obedience. To this strange remnant of rebellion he was proceeding to apply himself . . . when the mistress of the house rising to lead away the ladies from the table . . . it became suddenly apparent to every eye that the worthy orientalist had been most laboriously stowing away, into the capacious receptacles of his own habiliments, the snowy folds of a lady's gown, belonging to his next neighbour, and so voluminously, that a very small portion of it, indeed, remained for the lady's own use; the natural consequence of which was, of course, that the lady appeared almost inextricably yoked to the learned theologian, and could not effect her release, until after certain operations upon the vicar's dress, and a continued refunding and rolling out of snowy mazes upon snowy mazes, in quantities which at length proved too much for the gravity of the company. Inextinguishable laughter arose from all parties . . . until he had paid up the last arrears of his long debt. . . .

Thomas de Quincey,
Recollections of the Lakes and the Lake Poets, 1834–5

Festive Occasions

Well-known and traditional festivals were not always as they are today. In late eighteenth-century Wales, Christmas began at between 3 a.m. and 6 a.m. on Christmas morning with a religious service called plygain *(or* Plugen *in the following extract). This was preceded by supper parties in large houses, and in humbler homes by decorating the house and making treacle-toffee* (cyflaith).

Mrs Elizabeth Baker in her diary written between 1778 and 1786 says:

I set forth to celebrate what is named *Plugen*. . . . The table was spread with all the season produced – fish of every sort, Grows [grouse?], Fruits in abundance, especially melons.

Coffee and tea commenced it with an abundance of Wiggs [bun or small cake made of fine flour], buttered Pikelets and cakes. . . . The cards continued till supper which was a hot and plentiful one and resumed again after; about three in the morning coffee and tea etc., was again served . . . and after that was mulled Ebillon, and warm Punch for the males. The cards ceased. . . . The bell summoned us to Church; . . . prayers were begun, and the Church quite filled where we stayed till eight and broad daylight, hearing the different carols sung.

As Sub-Warden of New College, Oxford, Parson Wood-forde orders the Christmas dinner in 1773.

We had for dinner, two fine Codds boiled with fryed Souls [*sic*] round them and oyster sauce, a fine sirloin of Beef roasted, some peas soup and an orange Pudding for the first course, for the second we had a lease of

Wild Ducks rosted, a fore Qu: of Lamb and sallad and mince Pies. We had a grace cup before the second course brought by the Butler to the Steward of the Hall who was Mr Adams a Senior Fellow, who got out of his place and came to my chair and there drank to me out of it, wishing me a merry Xmas. . . . After the second course there was a fine plumb cake. . . . I supped etc., in the Chequer, we had Rabbits for supper rosted as is usual on this day. . . .

On Christmas Day one ate home-made puddings, pork-steak, goose (stuffed with potatoes), beef, home-made currant cake, and baker's currant cake for tea. There were no traditional occurrences associated with the Christmas dinner. The drinking of tea, whiskey, wine and porter was regarded as part of the Christmas celebration. Punch drinking took place at night. Any person calling to the house, or a neighbour passing the house was called in and got 'treated'. Some puddings and pork-steak were generally distributed too, from persons in the neighbourhood.

From a record made by the Department of Irish Folklore, University College, Dublin, on Christmas customs in County Waterford early in this century

During the American Revolution a Thanksgiving dinner in New England was a rare treat.

All the baking of pies and cakes was done at our house, and we had the big oven heated and filled twice each day for three days before it was all done. Everything was good though we did have to do without some things that ought to be used . . . of course we had no Roast Beef. None of us have tasted Beef these three years back as it all must go to the Army, and too little they get poor fellows. . . . [We had] a vegetable which I do not believe you have yet seen. Uncle Simeon had imported the seeds from England just before the war began, and only this year was there enough for table use. It is called sellery, and you eat it without cooking.

From a letter written during the Revolution, 1779

It seems very odd that celery was not known in New England in the eighteenth century, for it had been used in England since very early days. The cultivated kind was evolved from a wild variety called 'smallage' and was grown mainly by Italian gardeners in the late fifteenth and sixteenth centuries. John Evelyn (1620–1706), the great English writer, traveller, and gardener mentions it in his Salad Calendar and calls it 'the grace of the whole board'. It was, of course, at its best about Christmas time when it married well with the fine English cheeses, particularly Stilton which was first made about 1730.

The Oyster

Some foods from earliest times have had an almost magical quality, and have contributed greatly to the pleasures of the table. The oyster comes high on this list, and has figured in many epochs of the world's culinary history from mesolithic times, and perhaps earlier. Sergius Orata, about 100 BC, is believed to have started the first oyster farm in Italy.

It was a bold man who first ate an oyster.

Dean Jonathan Swift

Dean Swift's contemporary, the poet and playwright John Gay, wrote in a lighter vein.

> The man had sure a palate covered o'er
> With brass or steel, that on the rocky shore
> First broke the oozy oyster's pearly coat,
> And risked the living morsel down his throat.

Trivia, Book III

Many qualities apart from gastronomic ones are attributed to the oyster: it is said to be an aphrodisiac; the phosphorus content nourishes the body and the brain. Indeed Cicero has been described as 'nourishing his eloquence with the dainty'.

Around 1461, Louis XI of France decreed that the professors of the Sorbonne University should feast once a year on oysters, 'Lest their scholarship should become deficient'.

It is said that one of Napoleon's marshals ate a hundred oysters as a first course at breakfast.

Oysters are the usual opening to a winter breakfast . . . indeed they are almost indispensable.'

Almanach des Gourmands, 1803

In 1798 I was at Versailles as an emissary of the Directory, and had frequent dealings with the Sieur Laporte, who was secretary to the tribunal of the department; he was extremely fond of oysters and used to complain he had never eaten his fill of them.

I made up my mind to procure him full satisfaction

at last, and to that end invited him to dinner.

He came; I kept him company to the end of the third dozen, after which I let him go on alone. He went as far as thirty-two dozen taking more than an hour over the business, for the servant was a little slow in opening them.

Meanwhile I was doing nothing, and as that is an intolerable condition to be in at table, I stopped my guest when he was still in full career.

'My friend,' I said, 'it is not your fate to eat your fill of oysters today, let us dine.'

We dined; and he acquitted himself with the vigour and address of a man who had been fasting.

Brillat-Savarin, *La Physiologie du Gout*, 1825

In the nineteenth century oysters were cheap and within everyone's means.

'It's a wery remarkable circumstance, Sir, that poverty and oysters always seem to go together. . . . Here's an oyster-stall for every half dozen houses. . . . Bless it, if I don't think that ven a man's wery poor he rushes out and eats oysters in regular desperation.'

Sam Weller in Dickens's *Pickwick Papers*, 1836–7

She provided several courses of well-cooked fish, including perhaps a dozen oysters to each person as an *hors d'oeuvre*, which cost tenpence a head. . . .

James Bertram (1824–92) writing about Mrs Clarke of Newhaven, Scotland

Ernest Hemingway describes the restorative effect that oysters gave him after writing.

After writing a story I was always empty and both sad and happy, as though I had made love, and I was sure this was a very good story although I would not know truly how good until I read it over the next day.

As I ate the oysters with their strong taste of the sea and their faint metallic taste that the cold white wine washed away, leaving only the sea taste and the succulent texture, and as I drank their cold liquid from each shell and washed it down with the crisp taste of the wine, I lost the empty feeling and began to be happy and to make plans.

A Moveable Feast, 1964

... and of course they can also contain pearls!

The Truffle

The truffle comes into the same category as oysters: it is what Brillat-Savarin calls 'the jewel of cookery'. He also writes:

Whoever says 'truffles' utters a great word which arouses erotic and gastronomic memories among the skirted sex and memories gastronomic and erotic among the bearded sex.

However, Alexandre Dumas (père) says in Le Grand Dictionnaire de Cuisine (*1873*)*:*

The truffle is certainly not a positive aphrodisiac, but in certain circumstances it can make women more tender, and men more amiable.

Truffles were highly esteemed by both the ancient Greeks and Romans.

The Romans were as fond of truffles as the Greeks, and that is not saying little.

Martial, XIII. 50

The Athenians, enlightened appreciators of all sorts of merits, accepted with gratitude a *ragoût* with truffles, invented by Cherips. . . .

Athenaeus, Deipnosophistai

Maestro Martino in De honeste voluptate *insists that truffles should be first washed in wine and afterwards cooked under the ashes, and that they be served hot, and sprinkled over with salt and pepper: a recipe still highly thought of today.*

§

Truffles were plentiful in Rome, Greece, and Libya in ancient times, but then seemed to disappear from tables until the eighteenth century.

'Really, we have just eaten a superb turkey. It was excellent, crammed with truffles up to its beak, tender as a fat pullet, plump as an ortolan, fragrant as a thrush. To be sure, we only left the bones.'

'How many were you?' enquired someone curiously.

'We were two, sir!' he replied.

'Two . . . ?'

'Yes, the turkey and me.'

Alexandre Dumas, Le Grand Dictionnaire de Cuisine, 1873

The *reveillon* took place at the Marquise's flat, just a quiet, greedy supper with pounds of beautiful truffles quite plain, cooked under the ashes, of which Colette and myself ate an enormous amount. . . .

Marcel Boulestin, Myself, My Two Countries, 1936

Colette adored both eating and cooking truffles.

Once a year at home we had truffle-day. But, that could only take place if the bank account allowed, for Colette used to say: 'If I can't have too many truffles, I'll do without truffles' and she declared they should be eaten

[78]

like potatoes . . . it appears that cleaning them is an art and Colette would not entrust the responsibility of this to anyone else. You put half a bottle of dry champagne in a black stew-pan, with some bits of bacon fat lightly browned, salt and pepper. When the mixture boils you throw in the truffles. A divine and slightly suspect odour, like everything that smells really good, floats through the house. Under no pretext must the truffles leave the stew-pan, the scented sauce is served separately, hot in port glasses, and anyone who does not declare himself ready to leave Paradise or Hell for such a treat is not worthy to be born again.

Maurice Goudeket, *Close to Colette*

Caviare

Sturgeon and its sumptuous roe, caviare, is another of these magical foods with similar properties attributed to it.

Maestro Martino considered the 'chine of sturgeon delicately salted just as it reddens under the operation, the ne plus ultra *for an epicure'.*

In Greece, according to Athenaeus, the sturgeon was regarded as the best fish for a banquet. Alexandre Dumas, quoting Meyerbeer, says that caviare 'has the particular virtue of disposing the stomach to food. . . .'

§

Caviare is a Russian speciality although it is enjoyed by many races. However, in Russia, even today, it is within reach of many, and may form part of a zakouski *(hors d'oeuvre), or be eaten in between meals.*

Eat first, if you please, some egg patties with your soup, and then drink hydromel to wash them down, or else kvass. Pray take a little caviare, the roe of the sturgeon; fish soup you may prefer; cutlets, fowls, game, vegetables, are next at your service; and forget not to eat salt cucumber with your roast meat. What do you think of pig and curdled cream? And then apple bread or raw apples from the Crimea, or the Siberian or transparent apples, or the Kiev sweetmeat, or honeycomb or preserved rose leaves, or pickled plums. . . .

R. N. Bain, *Daughter of Peter the Great*, 1897

Jean de Reszke, the famous singer and teacher, loved caviare.

His knowledge of caviare was as world-famous as his B flat, and in the *salle à manger*, in his beautiful Paris home, there were always three little tubs of these precious eggs set in massive silver receptacles surrounded by ice.

The little theatre where we had our lessons was connected to the dining-room by a glass corridor. Here Jean would go hurrying along after a particularly trying lesson to snatch a spoonful of his extra-special grey caviare, which would sooth him as nothing else, and make him ready to face a nervous Aïda or breathless Parsifal. On very rare occasions when I managed to satisfy *Le Maître*, I was taken along this almost sacred passage, and given a spoonful myself. *'Voilà Petite Juta,'* he would say with an enchanting smile, 'Your Tosca has certainly earned you the food of the Gods today!'

Lady Luia Forbes, *Dinner is Served*

CAVIARE

The caviare was perhaps rather overwhelmed by the table decoration at the newspaper magnate William Randolph Hearst's dinner party in New York.

My most vivid memory of Hearst's dinner party was the table decoration which confronted me when I took my seat. It consisted of an entire stag, tastefully arranged athwart the table cloth. The interesting thing about this somewhat bizarre aid to digestion was that I was not even aware of the stag until the end of the first course which, needless to say, was caviare – grey, Beluga caviare, served by the bucketful.

Apart from the caviare I can only recall one item on the menu – terrapin. This was a very rare form of North American turtle which, as I was later informed, was colloquially known as the diamond-backed turtle – a suitable appelation. George Gershwin, leaning towards me and speaking *à haute voix*, informed me that it cost twenty dollars a portion, which I can well believe, for it was the most delicious thing I have ever tasted. I had never had it before, have never had it since, and doubt whether I shall ever have it again.

Beverley Nichols, *Down the Kitchen Sink*, 1974

A glass (or glasses) of ice-cold vodka is usually served with caviare and the first course, and this is not unlike the way calvados is drunk in Normandy as a digestif.

[We eat] *bouillon* and *pot-au-feu*, after which a glass of wine is taken, then tripe; then leg of mutton. Here a halt is called for the *trou Normand* [glass of calvados]. We fall to again with roast veal, then fowl, then the desserts, coffee, and again calvados.

Curnonsky, *A Guide to Eating in Normandy*

The Social Occasion

It must never be forgotten that the company, conversation, and ambiance *are as important, and on occasions, more so, than the food. Norman Douglas in* Siren Land, *written between 1908 and 1909, evokes this feeling to perfection, writing of meals in an old farmhouse in Sant' Elia.*

... I have memories of certain impromptu luncheons – quails and cream cheeses, and succulent raisins preserved in vine-leaves – on that upper loggia with a civilized and charming companion; memories of blue sea shimmering through a silvery network of olive branches, with talks, over coffee, of far-away things. ...

Thackeray points out the importance of one's surroundings to the enjoyment of a meal when dining at the Salthill Hotel, Kingstown (now Dun Laoghaire) in Dublin, in the 1840s.

In fact, in placing his banqueting-house here, Mr Lovegrove had, as usual, a brilliant idea. You must not have too much view, or a severe one, to give a relish to a good dinner; nor too much music, nor too quick, nor too slow, nor too loud. Any reader who has dined at a *table-d'hôte* in Germany will know the annoyance of this: a set of musicians immediately at your back will sometimes play you a melancholy polonaise; and a man with a good ear must perforce eat in time, and your soup is quite cold before it is swallowed. Then, all of a sudden, crash goes a brisk gallop! and you are obliged to gulp your victuals at the rate of ten miles an hour. And in respect of conversation during a good dinner, the same rules of propriety should be consulted. Deep and sublime talk is as improper as sublime prospects. Dante and champagne (I was going to say Milton and oysters, but that is a pun) are quite unfit themes of dinner-talk. Let it be light, brisk, not oppressive to the brain. Our conversation was, I recollect, just the thing. We talked about the last Derby the whole time, and the state of the odds for the St. Leger; nor was the Ascot Cup forgotten; and a bet or two was gaily booked.

The Irish Sketch-Book, 1843

England could also produce elegant surprises:

But I can remember once in England in a fairly Victorian household, and in spite of the year (1936 or so) being served, at the end of dinner which began with plovers' eggs, a kind of cold appetizer-tickler, rather a change from the usual hot, overspicy British fillip to a good meal. They were little coffins, as Elizabethan manuals would have named them, of rich pastry, generously filled with black caviare, and with one trimmed handsome oyster resting upon each dark bed. What a strange and intrinsically stimulating flavour at the end of the rococo menu!

M. F. K. Fisher, *An Alphabet for Gourmets*, 1949

A 'concourse of various excellences' was consumed by André Simon, the Hon. Harold Nicolson, Sir Hugh Walpole, and A. J. A. Symons, at Boulestin's restaurant, Covent Garden, on 10 February 1938, the hosts being X. M. Boulestin and Francis Toye. It consisted of:

Lamproie Bordelaise
Rôti de Porc Perigourdine, Pommes Parisienne
Salade de Pissenlit â l'huile de Noix
Fromage
Tarte de Famille

* * *

Château La Lagune 1922
Château Ausone 1914
Château Climens 1929
Fine Champagne 1830

André Simon says this of the lampreys:

Presented in a rich, dark, wine sauce, the succulent and boneless lamprey had a consistency midway between the sweetbread and the turtle-fin, with a delicate taste in which the sea played little part. But where is the vocabulary for taste? . . . I must content myself . . . by saying that it was one of the most delicious dishes I have ever eaten.

And of the rest of the menu:

Next came the principal course, a speciality of our host's province: melting-tender, symmetrical circles of roast pork, with a centre piece of truffle, and an undertaste of garlic and the jellified gravy from the joint. M. Boulestin had spent three hours that morning at work on this masterpiece of seeming simplicity. . . .

The Ausone of 1914 was a magnum. Light, yet well-balanced, aromatic, smooth and yet *brisk*, it was a wine perfectly suited to be the benignant dictator at luncheon. . . . The Camembert set it off admirably, and was itself admirable. The rind had been removed; instead, a coat of fine breadcrumbs comfortably invested it's tasty surface.

. . . the Tarte de Famille. But what a family his must have been if it ate such tarts! Imagine *crème brûlée* mounted in a *croûte*, lined with thin slices of fresh pineapple. . . . An Empress among tarts! And with it the most remarkable wine of the day . . . the Climens of 1929 . . . it has the honeyed sweetness and strength of complete maturity, the beauty of the blonde.

André Simon, *Food*, 1949

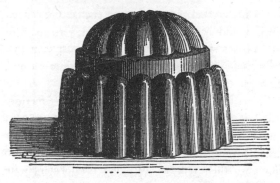

The rich sometimes indulge in eccentric fancies and the Twenties in England and Europe probably produced more unusual parties than any other modern decade. Beverley Nichols writes amusingly of two he attended.

Writing of colour takes me back to the parties of the Twenties – to Mrs Somerset Maugham in Chelsea, whose parties were always white, and to Elsie de Woolf in Paris, whose parties, as a rule, were predominantly red.

Both these ladies were inclined to carry their passion for their respective signature colours to extremes, particularly in the matter of food. Admittedly, Syrie's white interiors were exquisite . . . white walls, ivory satin curtains, white china vases filled with giant white enamel Chinese camellias, white leather chairs, white sheepskin rugs.

But when these principles were applied to the food, the result was less satisfying, though for sheer audacity Syrie got full marks. Her first white food party is very clear in my memory. On the buffet were towering mounds of white grapes, lit by the glow of tall white candles. There were cold chickens in a white glaze and poached soles with a white sauce. There were white endive salads, and sparkling meringues, and white peppermint creams in white Meissen trays. There were even white crystallized violets – an enchanting conceit which would have enraptured Ronald Firbank. But with all this whiteness, and a curious suspicion that one's inside was being subtly but surely white-washed, one began to long for a bloody steak.

With Elsie de Woolf – Syrie's Franco-American rival – it was the other way round. Everything that could possibly be red was red. Even the lobsters were turned upside down on the crimson table-cloths to emphasize their redness. Flanking the lobsters were joints of very sanguinary beef, carved by decorative young valets in scarlet waistcoats. The salads were of an exceptional redness – beetroot and tomato and red cabbage with a sauce tinted with cochineal. (This sounds disgusting; in fact it was delicious.) And all the wines, needless to say, were red. . . . And yet, as in the case of Syrie, one began to be bored by the redness, and even as one dipped an out-of-season strawberry into a concoction based on cherry brandy – (equally delicious) – one found oneself longing for a bright yellow banana, which one could take out of the room and peel in the conservatory, accompanied by a young person whose complexion, hopefully, would be firmly pink.

Beverley Nichols, *Down the Kitchen Sink*, 1974

§

The pleasures of the table were severely restricted during World War II, and Europe was slow to recover. It is doubtful if the gigantic meals of the past will ever be eaten again.

Alexandre Dumaine, the inspired French chef-proprietor of the renowned Hôtel de la Côte d'Or at Saulieu, who died in 1954, remarked: 'La grandeur, l'âme de la cuisine, est la simplicité.' He also said:

It is much better that the housewife contents herself

in perfecting unpretentious dishes. And that in itself is not always easy.

Alexander Watt in The Art of Simple French Cookery *(1962) writes:*

When we last called on Monsieur and Madame Dumaine we were invited to partake of a 'simple' lunch. By general standards this was far from simple fare, yet the main dish, a *Poularde au Vapeur du Pot-au-feu*, in its actual preparation, was certainly not complicated and can be prepared by any cook who has the time and the patience to do so. . . .

Rosa Lewis, the remarkable cook and owner of the old Cavendish Hotel in Jermyn Street, London, had some forthright views as to why some people's cooking is better than others.

Some people's food always tastes better than others, even if they are cooking the same dish at the same dinner. Now I will tell you why – because one person has much more life in them – more fire, more vitality, more guts – than others. A person without these things can never make food taste right, no matter what materials you give them, it is no use. Turn in the whole cow full of cream instead of milk, and all the fresh butter and ingredients in the world, and still that cooking will taste dull and flabby – just because they have nothing in *themselves* to give. You have got to throw *feeling* into your cooking.

from Mary Lawton, *The Queen of Cooks – and some Kings*, 1925

§

You have dined superlatively. The cognac glows in your glass. You stand in the mellow evening on the terrace of Miller Howe.

Sailing boats cut without a sound across Windermere, below and before you. A light breeze laden with the perfumes of the garden and meadows beyond, brushes the trees around. . . . It's a fair definition of happiness.

A guest at Miller Howe Hotel, Windermere, 1974

To return once more to the past ; Talleyrand said that two things are essential in life, 'to give good dinners, and to keep on fair terms with women'.

And let the wise and amiable Thackeray close the book:

Next to eating good dinners, a healthy man with a benevolent turn of mind, must like, I think, to read about them.

✐Acknowledgements

The editor and publishers gratefully acknowledge permission to use copyright material in this book:

Henri Bosco: Extract from *Barboche*, trs. Gerard Hopkins (1957). Reprinted by permission of Oxford University Press.

Marcel Boulestin: Extract from *Myself, My Two Countries*. Reprinted by permission of A. D. Peters & Co. Ltd.

K. Chang: Extract from *Food in Chinese Culture*. Reprinted by permission of Yale University Press.

Lady Luia Forbes: Extract from 'Dinner is Served' in *Food* (ed. André Simon, 1949). Reprinted by permission of Burke Publishing Co. Ltd.

Dorothy Hartley: Extract from *Food in England* (1954). Reprinted by permission of Macdonald Futura Publ. Ltd.

Ernest Hemingway: Extract from *A Moveable Feast*. Copyright © 1964 by Ernest Hemingway Ltd. Reprinted by permission of Jonathan Cape Ltd. on behalf of the Executors of the Ernest Hemingway Estate, and Charles Scribner's Sons.

Revd. Francis Kilvert: Extract from *Kilvert's Diary*, edited by William Plomer. Reprinted by permission of Jonathan Cape Ltd, on behalf of the editor and The Estate of Mr F. R. Fletcher.

Giuseppe di Lampedusa: Extracts from *The Leopard*. Copyright Feltrinelli, Milan 1958. Reprinted by permission of Collins Publishers, and Giangiacomo Feltrinelli Editore.

Beverley Nichols: Extract from *Down the Kitchen Sink* (1974). Reprinted by permission of W. H. Allen & Co. Ltd., and Eric Glass, Ltd.

André Simon: Extract from *Food* (Pleasures of Life Series, 1949). Reprinted by permission of Burke Publishing Co. Ltd.

Cornelia Otis Skinner: Extract from *Elegant Wits and Grand Horizontals*. Copyright © 1962 by Cornelia Otis Skinner. All rights reserved. Reprinted by permission of International Creative Management, New York.

Carol Truax: Extracts from *Father Was a Gourmet* (1965). Copyright © 1960, 61, 62, 63, 65 by Carol Truax. Reprinted by permission of Harold Ober Associates Ltd.

Joseph Vehling: Extract from 'Apicius: Cookery and Dining in Imperial Rome' in *Food* (ed. André Simon, 1949). Reprinted by permission of Burke Publishing Co. Ltd.

ACKNOWLEDGEMENTS

Alexander Watt: Extract from *Simple French Cookery* (1962). Reprinted by permission of Doubleday & Co. Inc.

While every effort has been made to secure permission, we may have failed in a few cases to trace the copyright holder. We apologize for any apparent negligence.

The illustrations in this book were taken from J. Gouffé, *Le Livre de Cuisine* (Paris, 1881). Courtesy of Alan Davidson.

Index of Authors